GROWING
the AFRICAN
AMERICAN
CHURCH

GROWING
the AFRICAN
AMERICAN
CHURCH

EDITED BY
CARLYLE FIELDING
STEWART III

Abingdon Press
Nashville

GROWING THE AFRICAN AMERICAN CHURCH

Copyright © 2006 by Abingdon Press

All rights reserved.

No part of this work may be reproduced or transmitted in any form or by any means, electronic or mechanical, including photocopying and recording, or by any information storage or retrieval system, except as may be expressly permitted by the 1976 Copyright Act or in writing from the publisher. Requests for permission should be addressed to Abingdon Press, P.O. Box 801, 201 Eighth Avenue South, Nashville, TN 37202-0801.

This book is printed on acid-free paper.

Library of Congress Cataloging-in-Publication Data

Growing the African American church/ edited by Carlyle Fielding Stewart.
   p. cm.
   ISBN 0-687-49839-2 (binding: pbk., adhesive perfect : alk. paper)
   1. African American churches.   2. Church renewal.   3. Church growth.   I. Stewart, Carlyle Fielding, 1951-

   BR563.N4G76 2006
   254'.508996073—dc22

                            2006019293

All scripture quotations unless noted otherwise are taken from the *New Revised Standard Version of the Bible,* copyright 1989, Division of Christian Education of the National Council of the Churches of Christ in the United States of America. Used by permission. All rights reserved.

Scripture quotation marked (CEV) is from the Contemporary English Version Copyright © 1991, 1992, 1995 by American Bible Society. Used by Permission.

Unless otherwise noted, Scripture quotations marked "HCSB" have been taken from the *Holman Christian Standard Bible* ®, Copyright © 1999, 2000, 2002, 2003 by Holman Bible Publishers. Used by permission.

Scripture quotations marked KJV are from the King James or Authorized Version of the Bible.

Scripture quotations marked (NIV) are taken from the HOLY BIBLE, NEW INTERNATIONAL VERSION®. NIV®. Copyright © 1973, 1978, 1984 by International Bible Society. Used by permission of Zondervan Publishing House. All rights reserved.

Scripture quotation marked "NKJV" is taken from the New King James Version. Copyright © 1982 by Thomas Nelson, Inc. Used by permission. All rights reserved.

Scripture quotations marked RSV are taken from the *Revised Standard Version of the Bible,* copyright 1946, 1952, 1971 by the Division of Christian Education of the National Council of the Churches of Christ in the United States of America. Used by permission. All rights reserved.

Scripture quotation marked AMP is taken from the Amplified® New Testament, © Copyright The Lockman Foundation 1954, 1958, 1987. Used by permission.

06 07 08 09 10 11 12 13 14 15—10 9 8 7 6 5 4 3 2 1
MANUFACTURED IN THE UNITED STATES OF AMERICA

CONTENTS

PART THREE: *Outreach*

PART FOUR: *Spiritual Formation*

PART FIVE: *Stewardship*

FOREWORD

Vance P. Ross

A black church growth resource is a particular gift for the Christian church. Our congregations yearn for this account of what has been done, the theology and principles that sustain it, and the persons God used to make it happen. This is a precious gift. It has been a long time coming. Thanks be to God, it is now here.

The black church has long needed documentation of its growth and possibilities. There have always been strong and growing churches. From Mother Zoar in Philadelphia and Living Springs fellowship recently begun in Mitchellville, Maryland, to the Kairos AME church in Nashville, Tennessee, to the New Life Church in Jacksonville, Florida, God raised and raises black congregations for God's glory and the salvation of humankind.

This has not occurred without substantial cost. African Americans stayed in the church as second-class residents in an institution that lost its way. The foremothers and forefathers bore the injury of a religion-inflicted bigotry for the noble purpose of a spiritual disturbance. Many left because of this. Justified by all that is holy, there were those who believed that ecclesiastically sanctioned bigotry, demeaning black humanity in the same manner as secular institutions, could be tolerated only at the price of disobeying God.

Others dared to stay. Those who remained assumed a holy posture as well: they chose to bear a cross, sacrificing their dignity as a witness to the resurrecting God. Their bearing of racist affliction resulted in a desegregated church. Albeit after much change in the secular arena, without the witness of these heroic men and women, the church in America could not claim diversity. Without their surrender to God's greater good, the justice-seeking assertion of this denomination would ring both hollow and false.

They are neither. In fact, critical to the truth of these has been the holistic evangelism of the black church. Black congregations have led the fight for justice and equity in this society while offering jubilant praise for God's amazing grace. Living in the denomination as resident aliens, these congregations have often been leaders in reaching persons with the saving message of the gospel. These congregations have believed God's blessing, chanced God's commands, and found themselves in the forefront of those who proved God's power.

Only a visionary pastor who has led such a growing congregation, a leader whose God-ordained vision is one for the whole church, could envision documenting this reality for the whole church. Only one who has done it and knows others who have done it could call pastors from across the nation to contribute to such a project. This is what characterizes Carlyle Fielding Stewart III. Dr. Stewart has been a "field general" for authentically Christian, flagrantly justice-seeking, and prophetically African American congregations for more than twenty years. He believed it could happen, preached and taught what God revealed to him, and that vision lives in a people called Hope Church. He saw it, witnessed God doing it elsewhere, and heard the call of God to assure that it was written as a testimony to God's faithfulness.

A scholar unparalleled in pastoral ministry, an evangelist of renown, and a teacher/preacher par excellence, Dr. Stewart dares to believe that the two so long divided according to Wesley—knowledge and vital piety—are essential to the black church. Because of this belief, he responded to God's call to document the proof of this belief. He knows that many yearn to believe that there are black congregations that significantly and successfully pursue God's call to the sacred commonwealth. This project is the result.

As is his custom, Dr. Stewart assembled for print only that which demonstrates excellence. The contributors herein have "made it happen" on the spiritual battlefield. Each church represented has grown spiritually and numerically and in its posture as a change agent. The communities they serve are better because these churches and pastors exist. These congregations and pastors model the best in that which God calls them to do and to be. They serve as teaching stations where other ministries can learn principles and practices for faithful ministry growth. There are no slouches here. These are among the best congregations for life change and soul salvation in this nation. Help and hope are mainstays where each of these congregations is concerned.

Note that while Dr. Stewart is a United Methodist pastor, the contributions found here cross the ecumenical spectrum. In the black religious community, religious affiliation never negates spiritual vocation. Difference in monikers does not disqualify or diminish one's gifts to the kingdom of God. The pastors gathered from around the black church have much to say to the whole of the black church, indeed, to the whole of the universal church.

Reading this book invites any leaders to journey to a place of immense possibility. Among those whose ancestors were enslaved, there is exceptional, divinely given optimism. Churches are making a difference, thanking God for the gifts of an overcoming heritage and a victorious future. These are the ministries amassed for this anthology. Read expecting to be blessed, anticipating God's moving on your ministry.

It has been a long time coming and now it is here— receive the empowerment, enjoy it, and be certain that you use it in your own ministry.

INTRODUCTION

Carlyle Fielding Stewart III

The past twenty years have witnessed an explosion of evangelism and church growth literature. Many of these writings provide useful frameworks and keen ideas for growing churches. Few, however, have been written by pastors who have actually grown churches in a variety of circumstances and conditions.

Moreover, much of this recent literature does not take into account the nuances of culture in constructing viable paradigms of church growth. Reading these texts, one is forced to ask, "How are the concepts and principles in growing churches from a particular cultural point of view relevant to my own cultural context, and how do they speak to the needs of the people I serve?"

For example, I may read a book that offers universal church growth principles that may theoretically and unilaterally apply to my ministerial setting, but how do I practically and usefully *translate* them into my peculiar cultural context? The savoir faire of practical application is often lacking in church growth literature, and some authors assume readers work from the same cultural frames of reference and thus will be successful in appropriating their models.

While there are many church growth ideas, strategies, and concepts that have universal appeal and applicability, they must have cultural relevancy and value if they are to be pertinent in different cultural contexts. What may work in an

Anglo church may not necessarily work in an African American church. What may work in a Korean congregation may not work in a Native American church. It is important that cultural characteristics of target audiences are taken into consideration when developing models of church growth.

It is also interesting how numerous approaches cited in church growth and evangelism literature often negate the importance of spiritual growth as an essential foundation to the numerical growth of congregations. Many strategies of evangelism presuppose that the necessary spiritual groundwork has already been laid in churches before they begin the crucial work of soul winning for Christ or that effective evangelism strategies can be implemented by giving only passing attention to matters of spirituality in growing and building strong faith communities.

Offered then are evangelism strategies that are more driven by Madison Avenue and popular culture than by bona fide Christian spirituality. Making people feel good is often more important in evangelizing persons for Christ than empowering their personal and spiritual transformation by giving them the proper spiritual tools. Nothing is wrong with appropriating current marketing strategies to attract people to a church. Popular culture can be a useful asset for assessing the needs and interests of a particular society and for determining what might "lure" or inspire people to join a church.

However, such strategies should not negate or obviate the importance of spirituality in creating a climate that will optimally enable people to grow spiritually. The more successful models of church growth stress the importance of developing a living, personal, spiritual relationship with

Christ. The invocation and participation of the Holy Spirit are basic elements in creating a climate of spirituality so as to ensure authenticity and long-term viability of the spiritual health of congregations.

Spirituality is thus essential in tilling the soil, planting the seeds, and reaping the harvest of effective evangelism.

It is also important to remember that not every congregation will boom in membership or burst at the seams with numerical growth, but every congregation can experience the spiritual growth indispensable to compelling members to become more faithful servants and disciples of Christ.

Sometimes in our efforts to grow churches, our primary concern is the number of members we can potentially gain versus the number of members who can be truly saved and transformed for the long haul. We become obsessed and driven by numbers. The membership growth of some congregations astounds us—how does any church effectively grow into and serve 10,000 or 20,000 members?—and while one applauds churches that experience such quantum leaps in membership, one wonders if the numbers are more important than the mandate to grow people spiritually.

I am not criticizing these congregations. Some churches have stressed the importance of spirituality, and that's why people flock to them. But not every church can or will grow into a megacongregation with membership in the thousands.

The idea that every church will grow into a megastructure is neither feasible nor plausible. Nevertheless, every church should and can develop ministries that will challenge people to grow in their awareness of Christ so as to be unabashedly empowered to witness that awareness with and to others in community. Every church can grow spiritually and numerically, but the numbers should not come at the expense of viable spiritual programs.

Churches *can* grow numerically and spiritually but spiritual growth is perhaps most important in understanding and sustaining the dynamics of all church growth.

The following document contains the testimonies and experiences of numerous pastors throughout the United States who have grown their congregations by employing various methods of evangelism. These pastors have lived in the trenches and have struggled to develop viable models of ministry that meet many needs and speak to different concerns.

Some pastors in this book are well known and others not so well known, but their work is worthy of notice. Some pastor megachurches; others, midsized churches; and still others, smaller churches. It's not the size of the church that matters but the quality of ministry that has been created and has enabled the church to flourish.

This volume provides information from African American pastors who have actually grown churches in a variety of different contexts. Many have built their congregations from nothing, and others were called or appointed to churches with viable members but grew their churches even more.

The common thread in all these offerings is indigenizing approaches to culture and spirituality that value both as viable constructs for ministry.

My prayer is that readers will glean valuable insights into church growth that will encourage and enable them to continue their labors in Kingdom building and soul winning for Christ wherever and whomever they are called to serve.

PART ONE

Evangelism

CHAPTER ONE

THE DOORS OF THE CHURCH ARE OPEN!

A LOOK AT EVANGELISM AND DISCIPLESHIP IN THE BLACK CHURCH

Tyrone D. Gordon

Traditionally, every Sunday the black preacher has issued an invitation that says, "The doors of the church are open!" It is an invitation to come to Jesus and then take Jesus into the world. That invitation has informed my understanding of the task of evangelism and discipleship in the church. The doors are open so that "whosoever will" can come in; they remain open so that the redeemed, transformed, and committed can go back out into the world for mission and ministry. Evangelism is not just about bringing folk in, but it is also the method by which we raise and produce prophetic disciples who go out and bring change and transformation to a world gone mad. Therefore, evangelism and discipleship go hand in hand to create a holistic approach that brings persons *into* a relationship with Christ *through* the church and moves

3

persons from simple membership in the church to Christian discipleship.

Dr. Zan W. Holmes Jr., my mentor and predecessor as pastor of the St. Luke "Community" United Methodist Church for twenty-eight years, always says that there is a difference between "growing" and "swelling." We are producing a generation of religious consumers who want to know what the Lord can do for them instead of committed disciples who ask, What can we do for the Lord? Not only are we called to bring folk in, but we are also called to help them grow into committed prophetic disciples of Jesus Christ. This has challenged me to take it upon myself to change the membership vows of The United Methodist Church. *The Book of Worship* of The United Methodist Church asks of new members, "Will you be loyal to The United Methodist Church and ... faithfully participate in its ministries by your prayers, your presence, your gifts, and your service?"[1] To me, that statement is membership producing—not disciple making. So we changed it to say, "I will be loyal to Christ through the church by upholding it with my prayers, my presence, my gifts, and my service." The emphasis is on discipleship, not membership! If we are loyal to Christ, we will be loyal to his mission. If we are loyal to his mission, we become his disciples. If we are his disciples, we will be loyal to his church!

The focus that has underscored my ministry for evangelism and discipleship is found in the Great Commission, or the Great Expectation, in Matthew 28:18-20 because this is not an option; it is the Lord's expectation. The Lord expects the church to grow and produce more disciples who will transform the world. This gives us the best balance for the evangelistic and disciple-making task of the church.

When the local church has a holistic understanding of evangelism and discipleship done in the tradition of the black church, it is prepared to reach out to all persons with the transforming power of the gospel of Jesus Christ and participate in God's plans to bring spiritual, political, social, and economic transformation to its community, the nation, and even the world. The task of evangelism and discipleship is to make the liberating power of the gospel of Christ become real in word and deed.

My church growth understanding is based on a cyclical view of the task of evangelism and discipleship. It is the cycle I call *reaching, teaching, training,* and *deploying.* It guides us from being a church member to becoming a committed disciple of Jesus Christ. This concept started forming while I was in my pastorate in Wichita, Kansas, at Saint Mark United Methodist Church and the church began to grow at an explosive rate. We had to come up with ways to keep persons from simply coming in the front door and exiting out the back doors. We wanted to encourage steady and constant growth and produce an active and empowered laity as well!

Reach Them!

In order to "make" disciples we have to go and "get" them. We must capture their minds, hearts, trust, and respect. We are called to be fishers of people, which means that we must cast our nets not our "lines" into the community. There is a difference between net fishing and line fishing! Jesus knew nothing about line fishing, but he knew plenty about net fishing. With a line all you need is a pole and bait, and you can pretty much choose which fish you want to catch. But with a net, all you can do is throw it out, and any kind of fish is likely to get in. It is not our job to decide which fish goes and which stays. A nonjudgmental attitude has opened the doors of our church so that all persons feel welcomed when they come through our doors, and persons drive for miles to experience that feeling of grace.

To evangelize and disciple African Americans, we must be culturally appealing by telling the old, old story in brand-new ways. We must be true to who we are. Our worship must be authentically black and socially relevant. We must be relevant for this twenty-first-century world where we are struggling for legitimacy. Throughout my practice of ministry, worship has been the entry point that fuels the growth in the church. Therefore, it is imperative that worship is geared to the first-time visitor and the *pre-Christian.* I prefer the term *pre-Christian,* which tends to be more positive than other terms, because I hate labels and it also speaks in faith saying, "You may not be a Christian now, but when we get through with you, you will be!"

In every worship celebration, we expect God to do something. We expect something to happen! We expect someone to walk down the aisle and make a commitment to Jesus Christ. All of worship is geared to that. When I was being interviewed to be the new pastor of Saint Mark United Methodist Church in Wichita in 1988, the question that I remember most is: "What do you expect to happen *if* you become the pastor of Saint Mark?" I vividly remember responding, "I expect that every Sunday, somebody will walk down one of these aisles and make a commitment to Jesus Christ!" Then someone shouted in the corner, "Well, good luck, Preacher!" God took that 350-member church to more than 2,700 members by the time we left in 2002! God works in the realm of anticipation and expectation. The same thing is going on at St. Luke "Community" in Dallas.

Music, liturgy, hospitality, and preaching are done in a way that persons who come in the doors will experience the presence of God in new and fresh ways and will be invited to make a commitment to Jesus Christ. Everything is done to reach persons with the gospel of Christ and through the love and hospitality of the community of faith. When folk walk in off the streets, they can fit right into place.

For evangelism and discipleship to be holistic to meet the needs of black folk, the black preacher must not only address the real, deep-seated needs of the soul but must also continue to be the prophetic voice, and the church must be the prophetic agent of change in our communities. No matter how middle and upper class we have become, racism, classism, and sexism are still running wild in our society. Black communities are in shambles, young people are at a crossroads, young brothers are incarcerated more than others, and folk need a word from the Lord that speaks to the issues of the day. We don't need any more motivational, "feel good" speakers in the pulpit. We need powerful preachers, women and men who are unafraid to be that prophetic voice in these challenging times.

7

The worship experience and the preaching moment must comfort, confront, challenge, and invite persons to come to Jesus. This relevant approach will attract those who have become disgruntled and disillusioned with the relevancy of the black church in today's world. We need churches and preachers who not only feed the flock spiritually but also challenge the societal ills with which the flock must deal on a daily basis. Anything less is cheap grace!

Teach Them!

I have long believed that good preaching and inspiring and celebratory worship can draw folk, but teaching will grow people. We will end up with shallow Christians with no commitment if we depend on what happens on Sunday mornings alone. A strong teaching component is attractive to those who are tired of church as usual. If we are reaching pre-Christians and not just transferring folk from one church to another, the teaching ministry of the church must be top notch to meet the challenge. Churches cannot grow disciples if no one teaches the traits of a disciple. That means we must be on the cutting edge in our Christian education ministries if we plan to be disciple training outposts in our communities.

In offering opportunities for teaching and immersing new Christians and growing mature Christians in the faith, we have had to place more emphasis on short-term classes. Christian education is a seven-day-a-week ministry at St. Luke "Community" designed to meet the needs of persons who have a lot going on in their lives and must make the most of their time. Our classes have become so attractive that persons from other churches and denominations have participated in them.

What makes St. Luke "Community" so attractive to thousands within the Dallas-Fort Worth metroplex is that we feed the mind and the soul. Not only do we offer times of revival for the spirit, but we also offer an annual lecture series that stimulates the mind. Our Zan Wesley Holmes Lecture Series has attracted some powerful personalities in the black Christian community, such as Dr. Jeremiah A. Wright Jr., Dr. Carlyle Fielding Stewart III, Dr. Renita Weems, Dr. Michael Eric Dyson, and the Reverend Emmanuel Cleaver II, to name a few.

Our Christian education ministries prepare all persons from the youngest to the oldest for discipleship in the community and the world. It is expected of every ministry and class to be part of some outreach ministry. We feel that one of the roles of Christian education is not simply to impart information but also to give inspiration to go beyond the walls of our sanctuaries so that the Word can become flesh once again.

In any respect, the teaching ministry of the church goes hand in hand with the evangelistic mandate because through it, one sees what God requires, who Jesus is, and what he taught that one grows and matures into a disciple. It is through the teaching ministry that the vine of evangelism is watered, cared for, and pruned so that it will grow and bear fruit for the Kingdom. The teaching ministry lays out the practical application of the Word and helps us understand more fully the Christ who liberates the oppressed, opens the eyes of the blind, and sets at liberty those who were bound. It helps us see the Christ who desires a personal relationship with us and expects us to be the agents of change and transformation in the world.

Train Them!

Training is a vital component in the continued and steady growth of the church and is an extension of the teaching ministry of the church. I believe one of the primary ministries of the staff, both lay and clergy, is to equip and empower the saints for ministry. If a staff person is doing all the work, then that staff person is not doing his or her job to equip and empower others for leadership and ministry.

Great care should be given to how we train not only new members but also existing members and the leadership team. The training of the leadership team is the key; it is they who make the decisions that determine which way a church will go. Properly equipped leaders will have a healthy outlook on the evangelistic and disciple-making task of the church.

What has helped support our growth is a leadership team that continues to challenge itself to walk by faith and not by sight. A team that is exposed to the best will come to expect and work for the best. The team must be trained so that living and operating within the mission and vision of the church become second nature. We invest time and energy in raising and developing spiritual leaders.

The call to leadership is not a call to a role of power but a call to move others into finding their place in the body as disciples of Jesus Christ. The leadership team is to partner with the pastor in keeping the church focused on the main thing: *making disciples for Jesus Christ!* So often, the church gets bogged down in minor things and forgets the major reason for its existence. We are so busy doing *church work* that we forget *the work of the church!* The main thing is to proclaim the gospel of Jesus Christ and invite others into a relationship with him and send them out into the world to bring spiritual, social, political, and economic change and transformation to our communities. We proudly invest time, resources, and training in the development of our leadership, and we take great care in raising up new leaders.

Leadership has been a key for the continued growth of the church! Our leaders were the ones who carried the ball, put flesh on the vision, and helped fight the battles to place the church in a position of growth. I cannot overstate the importance of a dedicated team whose members see themselves as the spiritual leaders of the congregation.

I always keep an eye out for persons who have leadership potential. Then I invite those persons to attend a special Bible study class that I lead along with an associate pastor of our church. We call it *Spiritual Leadership 101*. In it we go into depth biblically on what it means to be a spiritual leader in the church, how to behave as a spiritual leader, and what role a spiritual leader plays in the ongoing interpretation of the mission and the vision of the church. They leave the class with a heart for Christ and a heart for the church, and they are clear on the holistic mission of the church.

Nothing could have ever been accomplished without the Lord and faithful, committed, dedicated servant spiritual leaders who could see the dreams and visions and sense the new move of God in our midst. That became possible because in every way we have always believed in investing in them, exposing them to new ministries and new ideas, and training them in knowing what it means to be a servant spiritual leader in the body of Christ. When the leaders and the pastor are on the same page, evangelism will take place and more disciples will be made.

Deploy Them!

The best evangelistic tool is other disciples who go out and make an impact upon the world and in the lives of others. The early church in the book of Acts had a reputation of being the ones who turned the world upside down. We are called to turn the world upside down and then turn it right side up! We are not just to sit in our sanctuaries shouting how blessed we are. We are to ask God to take us into the areas where God is blessing. One of our members, Mrs. Shirley Isom-Newsome, always says, "we are blessed to be a blessing!" So once we reach them, teach them, and train them, we deploy them! It is time to send them back into the world to reach others and bring them in so that the cycle and the process continue. It is impossible to be a disciple of Jesus Christ without taking that love and using it to influence the lives of others and transform society. There simply must be a connection with all of the celebration of Sunday with what we do Monday through Saturday!

There must be an organized plan to send disciples back into the world to model the life of the Great Liberator, Jesus Christ. The black church of the twenty-first century must reexamine itself and make a decision about whether it will be more concerned with its "in-reach" or its "out-reach." We have made a conscious decision to focus on our "out-reach." We are proclaiming the gospel not only in word but also in deed. Our communities, our young people, and the brothers on the corner are looking at what we do more than listening to what we say. The old adage is true: *what you do speaks so loud that I can't hear what you say!* Sometimes that is a better witness to the transforming power of Christ than anything that we may say with our mouths.

We need disciples who can put into practice what they claim to have in their hearts. African American slaves put it like this: "If you've got good religion, you ought to show some sign!" The historical black church had one hand reaching up to God and the other reaching out into the world. That is the image we need to reclaim. We have retreated from the battlefield and left those in the inner cities to fend for themselves, yet discipleship requires that we live lives that love God with all that we are and our neighbors as ourselves. We have bought into the gospel of prosperity and have forgotten that there is always a cross before the crown.

Deploying the people into the world is designed to address the prevailing issues that plague our communities and to eliminate those barriers that hinder black America from reaching her divine potential. We work hard to help people dealing with shattered dreams, underfunded schools, the AIDS/HIV epidemic, the criminal justice system, poverty, homelessness, low self-esteem, self-hatred, unemployment, inadequate housing, and the like by dispatching disciples so that the Word becomes flesh and dwells among us. What a witness to the transforming power of the liberating gospel of Jesus Christ! Deploying the saints into the community and the world is more powerful than standing on street corners with tracts or knocking on doors on Saturday morning! When folk see that the church has the community at heart, the community will hold that church to heart.

From my understanding of the gospel, this is discipleship at its best. Hands that become Christ's hands; eyes that become his eyes; ears that become his ears; feet that become his feet. Discipleship is not some abstract concept but a lifestyle of servanthood that liberates the oppressed, sets the captives free, and opens the doors of the church so all are welcomed and *anyone who calls upon the name of the Lord shall be saved!*

As was earlier stated, it is a requirement that every ministry, every class, and every Bible study group be involved in some kind of outreach project or ministry that causes the Word to become flesh once again. We believe this is a part of the disciple-making process. Our witness to the liberating power of the gospel cannot be relegated to a couple of hours on Sunday morning. It must be a 24/7 lifestyle! It helps us understand that discipleship and evangelism are a lifestyle. We are equipping people to live out their faith in any setting, at any time, and in every way.

When folk are excited about their church, they can't help going out and telling others about it. They become the "marketers" of the church. They become the witnesses that Acts 1:8 declares that we shall be! They become the best publicity the church could ever have. And guess what? It's free and won't break the budget!

When the people of God are released to live in the power of the Holy Spirit, a powerful change will come over them, the church, their relationships, the community, and the wider world. When the people of God are deployed, they will transform any arena of which they are a part because folk will know that they are the Lord's disciples because of the fruit that they will bear! Through the church, the gospel will be proclaimed, lives will be transformed, possibilities will be realized, and disciples will be made. Then the doors of the church will be opened so wide that anyone can come in and the church can also get out into the world with the liberating gospel of Jesus Christ. We will then sense the power of his promise: "And surely I am with you always, to the very end of the age." The invitation is now extended. The doors of the church are open, and whoever wills, let them come!

Note

1. *The United Methodist Book of Worship* (Nashville: The United Methodist Publishing House, 1992), 93.

CHAPTER TWO

FISHING WITH FLAVOR

UNTRADITIONAL EVANGELISM IN THE AFRICAN AMERICAN CHURCH

Sheron C. Patterson

With all due respect, we do not have to keep doing the same thing that we've been doing repeatedly. Change is a good thing; I suggest that change can even be a God thing too! Evangelism has been around for centuries and can benefit from a fresh tweaking. That is, we can go fishing for the unchurched in new and exciting ways. No, we don't change the message—Jesus still saves, but we can change how we disseminate the message.

Let me suggest evangelism through relationship ministries. I call this fishing with flavor because it combines evangelism with a highly relevant topic—relationships. Evangelism through a relationship ministry means confronting tradition that seeks to keep new ideas tightly boxed in and labeled "we've never done this before," "we've never had that at this church," or "that's not Methodist."

Why relationships? There is an urgency that defies calculation in our community. The urgency begs us to evangelize. How urgent is urgent? Most of the children in our communities will be born into single-parent families. You can find more of our young men in prison than on a college campus. The HIV virus that ravaged the homosexual community is now pandemic in the heterosexual community. In addition, male/female relationships are at an all-time low, evidenced by plummeting marriage rates and skyrocketing divorce rates. These dire relationship problems are choking the life out of us. The only answer is Jesus. When we infuse the gospel into our communities, it breathes life back into them. We can breathe again with Jesus all over us and in us. This is evangelism.

Persons caught up in these problems are the fish that we seek to net and bring to Christ. Let us be clear: all of them cannot be classified as the unchurched. Some have been in church and been turned off or even turned on by other church folk. When we go fishing for them, we are acutely aware of church baggage they may have, and our need not to reinforce stereotypes about church people.

We, who know the love of Christ, are compelled to evangelize. If, as one great theologian stated, evangelism is "one beggar telling another beggar where to find bread," then using Christ's love as the vehicle of evangelism is one person telling another person where to find the source of authentic love and how to experience it on many levels. I used this evangelism method in a five-year-old suburban African American church. The program did increase membership because it raised the church's profile in the community and it raised the church's esteem.

In 1995, God poured out the vision and inspiration to create and launch The Love Clinic—a contemporary, Christian-based relationship ministry for single and married persons. The vision came while I was deep in the bowels of a seminary library, pursuing a doctorate degree. God directed me to come out of the ivory tower and go into the streets where people were ready to hear.

This served as my evangelical call. I heard God say, "Broadcast the good news about my life-changing power." The words of Matthew 28:19-20 came alive: "Go therefore and make disciples of all nations, baptizing them in the name of the Father and of the Son and of the Holy Spirit, teaching them to observe all that I have commanded you; and lo, I am with you always, to the close of the age" (RSV).

"Go" meant move quickly or expeditiously. There was no time to waste on this precious assignment. "Make disciples" meant that people needed to be molded and shaped for the better. They needed something that would meet them where they were and would take them where God wanted them to be. My interpretation of this was to create an evangelical instrument that addressed relationship issues with contemporary flavor to attract people to Christ. The problems that plagued our community centered on failed relationships with each other and with God. People want their relationships repaired, and no one is more qualified than Jesus to do that. He has a reputation for having *healing hands*. People whose relationships had been reshaped by The Love Clinic had indeed met Christ in the process. They had been discipled and were ready to go and tell someone else about Jesus.

People are hungry for a nonjudgmental classroom that equips them to deal effectively with life. The Love Clinic is a classroom that gathers the scattered, dispenses relevant information about God and how God interacts in their lives, anticipates a desire for God from the people, and provides opportunities to get involved in church—joining, serving, attending.

I shared the vision with a small committee created to dream and design. Their task: how do they embrace the community with the excitement that comes when people discover that Jesus has a plan for their lives? This committee included dreamers, fresh minds, and veteran members who had a hunger for the unchurched. The name The Love Clinic came as a result of believing that Jesus is the ultimate healer of broken relationships. We believe that Jesus' healing should be accessible to all, and that the local church should be the site for the healing.

To implement this, we needed a comprehensive plan to go fishing—deep-sea fishing. We were challenged to move away from the shore and cast our nets into unknown, uncharted waters. We were doing something that we'd never done before. The centerpieces of the project were community-focused monthly relationship seminars, held every second Friday at 7:30 p.m. in the sanctuary. Monthly programs demonstrated to the community that we were intentional about our mission. We used the television talk show format, complete with dynamic host and a panel of people with strong testimonies of how God brought them out. We sprinkled prayer liberally throughout, inserted a time for the collection of an offering, and concluded with an altar call that invited people to know Jesus and join the church.

We had a fresh evangelistic idea, but how would we get the word out? A crucial evangelism mistake we in the church make is not having a strong presentation. We created a broad-based media/marketing plan that would meet people everywhere with flyers, the Internet, radio, television, and print.

Colorful, professionally designed flyers are not optional. The days of ragged, handwritten flyers are gone. Anything that your church presents to the public reflects your church. We positioned our flyers in places such as restaurants, hair salons, and fitness clubs. Placing a stack of flyers at a car wash is evangelism because you are spreading the good news of God. The church members who distributed flyers talked to the people they met on their way. They talked about the church and invited people. These members may not have been comfortable saying, "Do you know Jesus?" However, they were comfortable saying, "Come on to my church next Friday for a power-packed seminar."

The Internet is a profoundly helpful evangelism tool. Persons go online and gain access to innumerable sites that improve their lives. We created a website designed to bring websurfers to the monthly events and ultimately to bring them to Jesus. The site is attractive, easy to navigate, and helpful. We gathered e-mail lists from businesses, book clubs, sororities, and fraternities to reach out to persons across the city who never had heard of the church or seen one of the flyers. An e-mail invitation made a strong impact.

Radio, television, and print (newspapers/magazine) are also vital evangelism tools. We sometimes shy away from these if we do not have large budgets. Yet we discovered that the PSAs (public service announcements) could be highly useful to the Kingdom on a budget. With well-written and constant PSAs, the media in our city pushed our events hard and often. I suspect that they did not announce our events because they wanted to help spread the word about Jesus. They thought they were promoting a relationship seminar.

The Love Clinic topics touched people between the marrow and the bone. Cutting-edge seminar titles attracted people to the church out of curiosity and their need for healing. Our first event addressed unfaithfulness in relationships. It was titled "Who Is Cheating on Whom?" It created a buzz among the churched and the unchurched. The people began arriving at 6:30 p.m. for the 7:30 p.m. event. All types of people came because they'd heard about a church teaching about relationships. You see, we all have issues.

Once inside the doors, the people signed attendance sheets so that we could establish a relationship with them afterward. These sheets gave us means of communicating with them about other church events too. Friendly ushers showed them to their seats and put a bulletin in their hands. At 7:30 p.m., the choir began a few upbeat selections. The pastor came forth, prayed, opened the Bible, and presented the scripture that supported the evening's topic.

Then The Love Clinic ground rules were presented: understand that we all have issues, don't laugh at someone's problem because it may be yours tomorrow, and recognize that God is able to turn your situation around.

A preselected panel of persons gave testimonies on how God delivered them from the issue of cheating. One woman confessed that she dated only married men, but God healed her. A man shared that he was habitually unfaithful to his wife, but God changed him. These testimonies stirred the audience. Questions and comments erupted. During these highly spirited interchanges, something happened. We were in the house of God after all. The power of the Holy Spirit was released as people came to understand that they were not the only ones going through problems, and that God was standing by ready and willing to help them too. The pastor made concluding remarks about God's power and the altar, and the doors of the church were opened. People came forth to pray and to join the church. Afterward, comments like these were heard: "I never knew that church could be like this"; "I thought my case was hopeless"; and "I had given up on me and so had the world."

As our attendance increased, so did our boldness to evangelize with stronger titles. Our fierce topics included "Are There Any Good Ones Left?" "When Loving You Is Hurting Me," "Creeps and Silly Women," and "Jesus Is the Only High that You Need." The Friday night seminars continued for three years and made a significant difference in the life of the church by raising the church's esteem and the church's profile.

Church Esteem

Church esteem is the collective, self-community concept of a congregation. A church's self-esteem reveals a lot about a church's ability to evangelize. Church esteem can be measured in ways similar to self-esteem. The way a person walks, talks, and communicates (or whether the person wants to communicate at all) measures self-esteem.

Persons with strong self-esteem are concerned about their outer appearance; they usually have an upright posture and hold their heads high. If you look good, you feel good, and you can produce well. In a similar sense, churches with self-esteem grow. The members carry and conduct themselves in ways that demonstrate they are pleased with themselves and their church. I witnessed this as a result of the evangelism program. The congregation had a major church esteem boost. The members were on fire about the evangelism program. The members appreciated its relevance and adaptability to their lives and the lives of others. The members seemed to walk straighter and held their heads higher. They felt good about themselves and the power of God to reach and change the lives of others. They realized that they could evangelize! Evangelism was not out of their reach! Evangelism was something that United Methodists do! They also understood that evangelism is a gift to give and receive.

Raising the Church Profile

Once the monthly seminars started, the church's profile was raised in the community, which is synonymous with raising the profile of Jesus. People in the community heard the church's name in a new context. We were no longer "that stuck-up Methodist church on the corner." Rather, we became "the church with the relationship seminars." Going from negative to positive recognition is exhilarating. The church took a bold step forward in the name of Jesus because the members decided to tell somebody about Jesus. Profile raising is a part of evangelism because Christ commands us not to hide our light ("You are the light of the world. A city set on a hill cannot be hid," Matthew 5:14 RSV). We are sometimes shy or reluctant to let the world know about our programming. We don't want to appear to "toot our own horns." Yet if no one knows about our programming, it will languish.

Evangelism Phobia

Fishing with flavor means confronting evangelism phobia head-on. As a lifelong member of our denomination, I've noted that when the word *evangelism* is spoken, people will run for cover, eyes will glaze over with indifference, or arms will cross to let it be known, "You are not making me talk to anybody about anything." Just uttering the word *evangelism* to some is akin to cussing them out because they usually become offended, enraged, or agitated. As a result of evangelism phobia, we can be guilty of failure to go and tell somebody. Our inactions declare that we expect the unchurched to figure out on their own that we are a warm, caring church, invite themselves inside, pry open our folded arms, and press themselves into our lukewarm embrace. Hence, we have a reputation in the community for being cold, standoffish, and even boring. The word on the street is that we are the *silk-stocking, snobbish crowd.*

This image was indelibly placed in my mind years earlier while serving as senior pastor of an older church in the inner city. We were in need of a musician and ran an ad in a community newspaper. We received a handful of applicants. One applicant, a young woman dressed in a contemporary fashion, took on a totally opposite persona once she began playing the piano. She transformed from a modern-looking musician into an ancient funeral dirge pianist. Gone were her smile and energy. They were replaced with a slow, morbid, mournful musical performance and a frown. I asked, "Why the change?" She quickly and eagerly explained, "This is what Methodists want, right?"

Yes, evangelism has a negative reputation in our churches, but I want to put a new face on it. I consider evangelism a gift to those who give it and to those who receive it. The gift of evangelism liberates us from the bourgeois trap that constrains us to talking about the problems and condemning those with the problems, but not daring to do anything about the problems. The gift of evangelism frees us from being judgmental as well. Who are we to judge someone else's problems when we know that we have our own? The gift of evangelism won't allow us to turn our heads, turn to another station, or go to the other side of the street to avoid the problems. We must address the ills of our society.

Evangelism phobia based on traditional modes of evangelism is understandable to some extent. In the days of

Christ, the concept of fishing was common to all. Everyone did it or knew someone who did. Today, fishing can seem intimidating and unreachable—and even unnecessary for some. To remedy the evangelism phobia, let's revisit the words of Christ found in Matthew 4:19: "Follow me, and I will make you fishers of men [and women]" (RSV). Implicit in following Jesus is acknowledging Jesus as the leader of our lives. We must be submitted to him. It is not reversed. Our connection with Christ enables us to fish.

To help the congregation come to understand Christ, a strong Bible study was put in place, reinforced by Bible-based preaching from the pulpit. Evangelism phobia is also eradicated by believing like the disciples that it's safe to go into the deep. That's where lots of fish are found. We left the shore and never looked back.

I fish occasionally with my dad, and I've learned a few things about fishing that are applicable to fishing with flavor in evangelism.

- Fishers like to fish. They are always looking for opportunities to fish—morning, noon, and night. Therefore, the people who go and catch should have a genuine affinity for new believers. This is a special affinity built on the ability to accept people as they are, make no assumptions about them, and embrace them with an open heart. Nothing kills an evangelism project faster than people who do not like potential new members.

- Fishers should not be afraid of the hook. The hook is a piece of metal with a sharp point designed to puncture and hold onto the fish. The hook is virtually inescapable. Most of the time, once they are hooked, they are hooked. The same is true of our Savior. He is the hook. The truth that Jesus has a powerful love for us and came to earth to save us is the hook that we use to bring in new members. We cannot be afraid to put the hook out there and use it deftly by courageously telling others what Jesus has done for us.

• Fishers should know how and when to use bait. People and fish are smart. They do not want to be captured by the hook; that's why we use bait or lures. Bait and lures do not mean that the hook is insufficient. It means that some fish and some people need an additional incentive to bite. The fact that some people run from the church has little to do with the fact that Jesus loves them. It has more to do with the fact that people who claim to be Christians have hurt them or the church has done something painful to them. Or they may run because they've heard about our reputation for being hypocrites. If we use bait and lures like great programming, professionally generated publicity, and God-fearing, smiling congregants, we will be successful.

Are you ready to fish with flavor? Are you ready to create your own innovative evangelism program? Here are a few questions to ponder:

1. Is your congregation bound by tradition? If so, how will you free yourself?
2. Are there visionary persons in your church? If not, how will they catch the vision?
3. Is evangelism a four-letter word at your church? How can you change that?
4. What type of lure or bait will your church use?

5. Do you enjoy fishing?

Since its inception, The Love Clinic has expanded into national seminars, college tours, and summer camps for grades two through twelve. The book *The Love Clinic: How to Heal Relationships in a Christian Spirit* (New York: Perigee Press, 2000) is an *Essence* magazine best seller.

CHAPTER THREE

GROWING MEN INTO SPIRITUAL STEWARDS

Elston Ricky Perry

The old way of evangelism designed to win African American men to the church no longer seems effective. A Men's Day or Get the Men Out program will often produce, at best, temporarily increased attendance during Sunday worship or will fail altogether.

Why in these dire times when we need more strong black men to come to church, stand up and represent the strength, power, and souls of our people do we not see them in our pews in droves?

The answer? Numerous black men feel that the church is irrelevant to their real needs and that the church has almost become a mausoleum for dead worship services, a museum that archives and preserves the past, or a place to go only for rituals such as baptisms, weddings, holy days, and funeral services.

Many black men feel that the church is a place where they are obliged to go and sit with their families to make their families feel good, to find a new female friend, or to pay just enough fire insurance by quelling their guilt to keep from burning up in hell.

Today, men must be reached for Christ at a most fundamental level. Men of today are not readily prone to join clubs and institutions just because it is acceptable social practice or the "in thing" to do.

We need strong black men in our churches. The African American church could be light-years beyond its present status if more men joined and participated in Kingdom and community building through the church.

But in order for this to happen the church must create a climate of belonging; a place where men can feel at home and find inner personal meaning. The church must take responsibility in empowering men, and that empowerment can occur through programs that will encourage their stewardship.

In this chapter, I'd like to share some useful strategies in increasing male participation in your church. This information has been gleaned from fifteen years of pastoral experience in various churches in Florida and California.

The first part of this chapter will delineate *things we shouldn't do in trying to win men to Christ, which are the Five P's of turning men off*. We can no longer afford to run men away who have yet to make the connection to a church. The second part of this chapter will specify *the Five P's of connecting men with Christ and the local church*. The third segment will cite *how we keep men in the fold of fellowship in the church*.

Five P's That Turn Men Off from the Church

The following lists the Five P's that we should avoid in trying to reach men for Christ. Such strategies often do more to turn men away from the church than encourage them to belong.

1. *Pressure.* Most pastors and laity in leadership believe it is their appointed duty to get a man to sign his name on the membership roll's dotted line; close the deal; or make a public confession, acknowledgment, or vow-pledge to the congregation in public worship. Many men find this to be a turnoff and will stall, excuse themselves from the church, hedge, lie, or join—only never to return again.

Black men are under enormous pressure in our society, and coercion to join something feels in many ways like another heavy brick added to the load they are already carrying. Pressure tactics do little to help a man to develop a living personal relationship with Christ.

Rather than encourage a man to come to Christ on his own accord, strong-arm tactics to join the church turn him off and run him away. The pressure to join should be replaced by an open and special invitation to participate and belong to the community of faith.

2. *Politics.* Many men do not want to involve themselves in the politics or "politrics" of the church. If you go to a man who casually attends your church and cite to him why you need him to offset or support a political agenda, he will, for all practical purposes, bolt for the exit. Politics can be slippery business. Already seeking to escape the slime and grit of daily life, men can become disillusioned upon discovering that the church is political and that such politics can be even more cutthroat than the politics of the world.

Every church has a certain amount of politics. Ministry to God's people should never be mired or compromised by shadowy political processes. Black men are generally disillusioned with the politics and politrics of society with its unequal distributions of power, racism, sexism, and other strategies of oppression that "bind the strong man" and keep him enslaved. Shun the use of politics as a means of winning men to Christ.

3. *Promises.* Some pastors and leaders will make promises that cannot be kept just to get men to join their churches. Men of today hold the same principles and ethics of previous generations. One's word must be one's bond. They would rather you be honest and real with them about your present realities than lure them with promises that cannot be kept. The issue here is integrity. Don't make promises that you cannot keep. Promise to serve and empower them through the means available to you, but don't cloy and shower them with untruths that will in the end discredit your efforts. Promise to stand with them and help them through the storms and challenges of life, but do not give them false hope. Do not compromise your beliefs and principles. God does not need panhandlers in church.

4. *Promiscuity.* Are you trustworthy? Could a man trust you with his wife, niece, or mother? Men want to live a life of holiness. They want a church where people are walking the talk of holiness. Too many preachers have reputations as those who *prey on* women rather than *pray for* them.

By creating a climate of promiscuity through licentiousness, churches can often place innocent members in vulnerable positions that can later result in sexual harassment litigation and destroy the church's reputation.

Walking in holiness means possessing moral authority, which is essential in garnering respect and winning men to Christ in today's world.

5. *Prejudgment.* The last thing a black man needs is to be prejudged by his peers and others in the larger society. Various processes of devaluation and depreciation often exist that demean the personhood and power of black men. No other group in American society has had to contend with as many stereotypes, battle existing phobias, struggle against the foils and perils of racism, and vie for available material resources than African American males.

American society remains primarily racist, and although great advances have been made in race relations over the last twenty-five years, black men are still often shattered by the anvils of oppression through various processes of emasculation and dehumanization.

The church must dispense active spiritual antidotes to the poison of oppression. It must understand the promise and dilemma of African American men and work indefatigably to change their condition and the world in which they live. Prejudgments that support and perpetuate existing stereotypes do nothing to win men to Christ.

Five P's of Personal Connection

The question is, how do we connect our men to the one institution in the black community that still holds the greatest promise and potential for self-realization, advancement, independence, and interdependence for black people?

The answers are found in the approaches taken to bring them into the body of Christ. No two churches are identical. Strategies and methods of inspiring men to join the church are often *culturally conditioned, textual, and contextual.*

The church of today must be creative and bold in fashioning approaches that will speak genuinely to the needs of African American males. As leaders, we must be willing to pray and to seek God's direction. The hardest part is to *wait on the Lord*! Don't allow yourself to become the featured attraction. Remember, it is not about you; it is about God in relationship with each person.

The Five P's to personal connection are:

1. *Pardon.* Black men strive to shed the scoundrel image heaped upon them by the larger society and their own sinfulness. They need to know and feel God's love and experience God's grace in their daily lives. Pardon means forgiveness. Forgiveness means the capacity to look within and admit faults and mistakes so as to open oneself to God's redemptive possibilities. Forgiveness means opening those same possibilities to others to find healing and wholeness in life.

The world is adept at condemnation. Needed are mercy, grace, compassion, and forgiveness. To know and experience Christ is to experience such grace and mercy.

Men need to know that all have sinned and fallen short of the glory of God and that none of us is above reproach. They also need to know the meaning of salvation and that God's grace and love are unconditionally available to them. A pardoning church is ultimately a loving church. He who has been pardoned can also pardon others, and black men need this more than anything else in this world. Bringing men to Christ often means creating within the church a safe haven for pardon and redemption.

2. *Patience.* The road to spiritual success is perennially under construction. As God has taught us to wait, we must be patient with every man. Each man must look within himself to be certain that his decision is truly his alone. Personal transformation through Christ takes time. Often it is a gradual process by which each man periodically comes into awareness of God's grace. Sometimes the transformation can occur in a flash, such as Paul's Damascus road experience, or it can take years to develop.

As God is patient with us, we must learn patience in winning men to Christ. Many men are wounded and need time to heal. People who are hurting usually hurt others, and many men do not understand the depths or magnitude of their personal pain. Many are distrustful of others, particularly the church and preachers. They must be cultivated gradually, and only time can help them benefit from personal transformation. The church cannot afford to give up on black men. We must work fervently until the desired results are achieved, which are salvation and liberation, wholeness and wellness in Christ.

3. *Permission.* Men need permission to cry, permission to hurt, permission to heal, and permission to change their lives positively. Black men have been beaten down so long that in many cases it's an uphill climb to the bottom. In a society that has taken away an unbridled ability to soar the high winds of personal achievement, some men need permission to move ahead with their lives and find wholeness. The church becomes a place where men find the permission

to be whole and well, permission to succeed and conquer the horizons of life. In a world where his birthright has been stolen and his legacies trampled underfoot, the African American man must once again know that the God who loves and created him gives him permission to be a man and to offer something of value to his community and world. He does not need that permission from the larger society but must somehow reconnect with his Creator and Redeemer to know that he is a man and can achieve what he will in the larger scheme of life. This is his right as a man, and this is his spiritual birthright as a child of God.

The church must be careful that it is not part of the emasculation process of black men. In a world where his permission to be a real and true man has been taken away, the black church must cultivate a world where that permission to be who God called him to be is once again granted.

4. *Participation.* Too often in the church we create programs we believe will benefit men and then invite them to participate. Seldom do we survey their needs and then thoughtfully devise ministry opportunities that will speak to those concerns.

Give men the opportunity to participate on their own terms. Ask them how the church can be more meaningful and relevant. Seek their opinions on such matters, and consult them in the process of creating your programs.

Short-term outreach projects, Bible studies, workshops on prayer or stewardship, fellowship experiences, or opportunities for church service work best. Black men must not simply be the *objects* to whom the church's mission is directed but the *subjects, the co-intentional creators who partic-*

ipate in the church's mission to the world and to others in need. They must be moved from passive observers to active participants in building a viable world community. Participation means empowerment.

As men are encouraged to participate in a life of community building and empowerment, they are challenged to view themselves as active transformers of their society and world. By actively transforming their world, they can envisage themselves as meaningful, vital, and valuable. Personally transforming one's world goes far in revising one's self-image from powerless to powerful.

Invoke their participation. Challenge them to get involved in God's work by inviting them to participate in activities centered on their ultimate concerns as men and citizens of the community.

5. *Play.* Most men enjoy fellowship. Instead of competing with sporting events, include sporting opportunities in your ministry. Recreation is vital to wholeness and well-being. Golf clubs, bowling teams, walking groups, and other sports-related fellowship can help men to bond around common concerns and interests.

Inviting and Keeping Men in the Fold as Spiritual Stewards in the Church

All churches, particularly black churches, can use the help and resourcefulness of more men. Needed are men who are trustworthy, reliable, spiritual, loyal, faithful, grounded, respectful, and respectable. Once men have been identified and brought into the church, they can serve as armor bearers or spiritual stewards in the church's ministries.

Proverbs 27:17 reads, "As iron sharpens iron, so a man sharpens the countenance of his friend" (NKJV).

It is my belief that men win other men to Christ. When men find themselves connected to the church, they not only bring their families but they also draw other men.

Developing a spiritual steward involves not only awareness of the Five P's of the dos and don'ts with men but also the selection of men by the pastor and lay leaders in the church to serve in various capacities.

I have designed a seven-session training manual that has proved effective in several faith communities. At the close of each session if any man feels he is not ready or able to serve, he is free to step off for a time.

Neither time nor space allows me to explain the sessions in their entirety; the following is a brief description of the training manual for spiritual stewards. The manual is designed to teach, empower, and inspire men of good standing who willingly volunteer to undergo training necessary to serve as the second tier of spiritual leadership in a church. Each man must first pray and consult with his family before accepting this honor of service.

The formal training is divided into seven sessions that emphasize the areas of spiritual stewardship: *overview, prayer, visitation, Holy Communion and Holy Baptism, witnessing, lay shepherding,* and *commissioning.* Each session lasts a minimum of an hour and is led by the pastor or someone designated by the pastor.

Attendance at all seven sessions is required so that a bond of brotherhood is created among the candidates. Each candidate is to bring a Bible, training manual, and notebook, and he is to complete an assignment for each session.

The first session is the Stephen Session and addresses *the role and responsibilities of a steward.* The three Greek definitions of *steward* are *oikos, oikonomos,* and *oikonomia.* This session clarifies the distinction among trustees, financial stewards, and spiritual stewards.

This session includes the qualifications that, in part, are found in 1 Timothy 3:8-10. Each qualification is discussed in depth with contemporary illustrations accompanied by biblical examples and references. A spiritual steward is to be:

- Loyal to the pastor.
- Knowledgeable of duties and responsibilities.
- Faithful in his assignments.
- Faithful in attendance to church activities.
- Faithful in conducting daily private devotions.
- Faithful in his duties as a husband, father, son, and so on.
- Faithful in his financial support of the church through tithes and offerings.
- Able to comport himself in a way that glorifies God and edifies others.

The second is the Philip Session. Here *prayer* is the theme. Everyone must define prayer in his own words. Supporting scriptures are given, such as 1 Thessalonians 5:17, John 14:13, and Romans 8:26. The goal is for the candidate to learn the essentials of prayer and develop a genuine prayer life. Learning the importance and types of intercessory prayer is emphasized in this session as well as the "mechanics" of prayer.

Session three is named for Prochorus, and the theme is *visitation*. James 1:27 and Matthew 25:36*b* are the guiding scriptures for the session. Each candidate is to understand and respect the privacy and confidence of the members, families, and friends whom they will visit. The candidates are to learn the difference between a home and a hospital visit. They will also learn the difference between a steward's visit and a pastoral visit. The steward cannot and must not ever assume the role of pastor. In this session the candidate will learn the importance of being a good listener and less of a talker.

In the Nicanor Session, themes of the *sanctity of Holy Communion and Holy Baptism* are taught. Denominational theology, ritual, and guidelines informing these practices are reviewed. Each candidate is given the opportunity to share his understanding of these rituals. The pastor cites scripture references and explains them. A checklist and future assignments are shared.

In the Timon Session, the theme is *evangelism* and winning more souls, particularly men. The guiding scripture is Matthew 28:18-20, the Great Commission. Supporting scriptures are given, such as 2 Corinthians 5:11-20, Luke 14:25-35, and Acts 2:47.

Discussion covers the Five P's of connecting men to Christ, keeping them in the fold, and inspiring them to become good stewards. Discussion focuses on developing strategies of evangelism that are designed specifically to reach black men on various levels. The social demographics of black males within target communities, such as age, income, education, location, vocation, marital status, sexual orientation, and others, are presented. Role playing, practice strategies, and other methods are explored to train and equip men in the essentials of inviting and encouraging the participation of men in the church.

The Parmenas Session focuses on *lay shepherding* or *lay leadership*. Ministering to the needs of the faith community, first to the members and then to the entire community (Galatians 6:10), is discussed here. Upon completion of his three- to six-month training and probationary period, each steward will be given a list of members for whom he will have spiritual oversight. Models of servant leadership, the character and qualities of Christian servants, and other topics are explored in this session. The importance of being Christian models who will inspire other men and women to service is underscored.

The Nicolas Session capitulates and summarizes all previous sessions. It involves signing a covenant of service and concludes with a breaking of bread celebration and induction of the new stewards into the brotherhood of Christian spiritual service.

The following is an example of the covenant wording:

As a member in good standing of [Your Church], and as a man who believes in God the Father, Son, and Holy Spirit, and as a man who believes in the Holy Bible, and as a man who will uphold the teachings of our church, I promise to the best of my ability to live a life worthy of a Christian leader, and after prayer, reflection, and consultation with my family,

I hereby agree to serve as a spiritual steward of [Your Church]. I understand that if I should be found unworthy or unable to fulfill my duties as specified in the guidelines of spiritual stewardship, I will be excused from this honorable place of service without bitterness, opposition, or rancor by the pastor.

*Signed*_____

I have found that our primary failure is not equipping the saints for ministry. Ephesians 4:11-13 reminds us,

> It was he who gave some to be apostles, some to be prophets, some to be evangelists, and some to be pastors and teachers, to prepare God's people for works of service, so that the body of Christ may be built up until we all reach unity in the faith and in the knowledge of the Son of God and become mature, attaining to the whole measure of the fullness of Christ. (NIV)

If we are to win more men to Christ today, we must intentionally develop ministries that speak to their needs and encourage their participation in the church.

This particular model has enabled me to inspire scores of men into service at the various churches I have served. I have personally found that by increasing the presence of men and by equipping them to become spiritual stewards, the life and health of the local church were tremendously strengthened.

We must learn not to turn men off. We must discover their real needs, and we must create a place in the church where they can meet their own ultimate concerns as men through vital ministry to the people of God and the communities they are called to serve.

PART TWO

Preaching and Worship

CHAPTER FOUR

PREACHING AND WORSHIP IN THE AFRICAN AMERICAN CHURCH

J. Alfred Smith Sr.

Preaching and worship are part and parcel of each other, for preaching must have a contextual foundation for the preacher to stand and proclaim to hearers the spoken word and the Living Word. This Living Word is God incarnate in Jesus Christ, who on earth was fully God and fully man. In her wonderful book *Weary Throats and New Songs: Black Women Proclaiming God's Word*, preaching professor at Emory University, Teresa L. Fry Brown, describes preaching in a lyrical way. She calls it "Singing in the Key of God."[1]

Preaching in the African American tradition has a cultural distinctiveness and a historical uniqueness. I will endeavor to explicate and amplify this concept.

Black Preaching in Worship

A number of homiletics scholars write about the hermeneutics and homiletics of African American pulpiteers. Olin P. Moyd in his work *The Sacred Art: Preaching and*

Theology in the African American Tradition describes preaching as context and theology as content. The context of which he speaks addresses the creativity and artistry with which black preachers capture the heads and hearts of the hearers.[2] Dr. Moyd buttresses his thesis by quoting from highly respected Professor Henry Mitchell. Dr. Mitchell says in his well-written book *Black Preaching* that most of the best black preaching "maintains depth and relevance by means of art rather than argument."[3] In 1984 Broadman Press in Nashville, Tennessee, released my book *Preach On.* In this work, I endeavored to write about the artistic creativity of African American preachers who have used poetic language to make the gospel come alive. In my thinking, the best portrait of the uniqueness and particularity of black preaching is found in an out-of-print book called *Joy Songs, Trumpet Blasts, and Hallelujah Shouts.* This book was written by the wise pastor-scholar Carlyle Fielding Stewart III. He has Master of Divinity and Doctor of Ministry degrees from Chicago Theological Seminary and a Doctor of Philosophy from Northwestern University. Dr. Stewart believes that the four elements of black preaching might be called the four corners of the art. These four corners are poetic recitation, imaginative insight, spiritual pharmacology, and spiritual and social transformation. Dr. Stewart says that "the rhythms and fires of the poetic venue in black sermonizing both escalate and titillate the spiritual sensibilities of black believers."[4] He adds, "From the way the preacher begins his sermon to his orgasmic ascent toward the spiritual climax is all poetic adventure."[5]

In my classes on preaching at the American Baptist Seminary of the West and the Graduate Theological Union in Berkeley, California, I tell the students that preachers must have music in their souls, and that they must have rhythm to transport gospel melodies to a culture controlled by the noise of discord and dissonance. When Dr. Stewart speaks of black preaching as imaginative insight, he is speaking of the ability of preachers to illumine the ancient biblical text with picturesque language so that people will see with the eyes of their souls the message as it was in ancient times and also the relevance of the message for the here and now.[6] Black preaching as spiritual pharmacology is preaching that has a medicinal aspect of providing psychospiritual healing for souls wounded by a cruel world. The idea of black preaching as spiritual and social transformation has both priestly and prophetic dimensions. Hearers are challenged to grow spiritually and to live ethically and responsibly as true disciples of Jesus Christ. However, since the gospel is not only personal but also social, hearers are challenged to address societal evils and to worship for justice within the structures of society.

The black church was truly a prophetic church that challenged the status quo until the death of Dr. Martin Luther King, Jr. Black church historians have documented the stony road of our pilgrimage, and a classic on this topic is *Black Religion and Black Radicalism* written by Gayraud Wilmore and published by Orbis Books. Younger African American preachers who suffer from natal alienation because they have cut their cultural and ethnic umbilical cord are not aware of their historical theological roots of worship. Hence, their worship and preaching are entertainment centered. The emphasis upon personal and social transformation is missing. The preaching of the cross and the cries of human need are missing. Many popular radio and television preachers have no cross in their church auditoriums or worship settings. The significance of returning to the cultural context of black preaching is most important if the sermon will be what Dr. Stewart calls the "the apex of creative soul force in conjunction with the Holy Spirit."[7] I agree wholeheartedly with Dr. Stewart when he says:

> Black preaching then has healed lives, brought families together, comforted the afflicted, and afflicted the comforted, been a catalyst for cultural, spiritual, and social freedom, and black institution building, served as a force for the creative transformation of black communities, institutions, and the personal lives of African American people. No other medium has done more to help shape, interpret, and disseminate black claims and aspirations for black freedom than black preaching.[8]

The younger preachers are challenged to remember the prophetic preaching of their predecessors. They are called to preach to a postmodern generation of persons who either domesticate God into a harmless, benevolent deity or a glorified bellhop or dismiss God as being an artifact of a historical past that is irrelevant for the challenge of today. Younger leaders such as Oxford-trained Frederick D. Haynes III and mentors such as the famous Jeremiah A. Wright Jr. address this concern as their writings reinvigorate the justice agenda in the powerful book *Blow the*

Trumpet in Zion. This work should be required reading for all clergy and especially for all seminarians. I will be teaching this work in my classes on African American spirituality. I would also recommend that all preachers read *The Passion of the Lord: African American Reflections,* edited by James A. Noel, San Francisco Theological Seminary professor, and Pastor Matthew V. Johnson Sr., who holds a Doctor of Philosophy in philosophical theology from the University of Chicago and leads Christian Fellowship Baptist Church in College Park, Georgia. In this book, leading African American theologians and biblical scholars reflect on how Jesus' forsakenness resonates with the black experience and whether this suffering can make sense to young African Americans caught up in a culture influenced by hip-hop and the nihilism that Professor Cornel West writes about in *Keeping Faith* and *Prophetic Fragments.* In *Democracy Matters,* Dr. West challenges all preachers in describing the characteristics of the Constantinian Church in comparison with "the prophetic church." African American preachers who choose aping the bland conservatism of the religious right, according to Dr. Matthew Johnson, have become little more than a "grotesque caricature" of white evangelicals who have not shared the black experience of suffering.[9] Authentic worship is rooted in the social location of a people who live with the trauma of undeserved suffering and with the overimbalance of present-day suffering that has no visible redemptive value. The majority of black Americans are not upper-middle-class persons whose class status minimizes their degree of unjust and senseless suffering. Hence, the sermon, song, and shout of black ecumenical worship constitute a collective arrangement of empowering black worshipers to live triumphantly in seasons of good times and bad times. Let us consider how the rich diversity in black worship contributes to the creativity and aliveness of the black worship experience.

The Black Ecumenical Worship Experience

A serious study of black worship must consider the African foundations of present-day black worship. The African cultural traits have mingled with European, Asian, and American liturgical practices. As these cultural traditions influence each other, the black worship experience moves creatively into different styles, genres that work to always create the new. So in studying the metamorphosis of black worship one examines the camp meeting songs, black metered hymns, spirituals, anthems, Pentecostal music styles, gospels, praise songs, contemporary music, and even a hip-hop genre that appeals to masses of young adults of all races. Gospel music workshops that are held annually across America have featured Japanese gospel choirs. The African American gift to worship reveals the rich variety of denominational expressions. In addition to the numerous denominational hymnals that date from 1801, there is the African American Heritage Hymnal of 2001, which was edited by Dr. Delores Carpenter and Nolan E. Williams Jr. This ecumenical hymnal has litanies, scriptures, and 575 musical entries that are most useful for planning worship services to highlight the high holy seasons and special days of the African American ecumenical family.

Any student of black worship who seeks to develop expertise and competence in the field would do well to read the most comprehensive treatment of the subject in the book *In Spirit and In Truth,* written by Dr. Melva Wilson Costen and published by Westminster John Knox Press. People who read Dr. Costen's work will expand their understanding and appreciation of black worship. They will also learn about the theology of worship that is rooted in the Hebrew Bible and the Second Testament.

Much has been said about the sermon, song, and shout that constitute black worship. The music prepares the hearts of worshipers for hearing the preaching of the sacred word. The shout is a Holy Spirit motivation of praise and spiritual ecstasy, which acknowledges the goodness and presence of God. This mystical element of the presence of the God of holiness in the worship service makes worship authentic. Since the living God is present, worshipers are eager to praise this God as well as to pray to the benevolent and magnanimous Creator who sustains and invigorates those who worship in spiritual truth. Dr. Howard Thurman has much to say about the adventure of prayer: "The basic proposition underlying our need for prayer is this: We wish never to be left, literally, to our own resources. Again and again, we discover that our own resources are not equal to the demands of our living."[10]

Dr. Thurman reminds us that prayers provide us with spiritual resources for living these days and for facing the challenges of life. Prayer ushers us into the presence of the

God whom we praise and preach about. "He or she who speaks for God must speak to God and must listen to the voice of God. The servant of God is no stronger than his or her prayer life. In a world of turbulence, the one who communes with God has the secure foundation that can withstand the earthquakes of life."[11]

It has been said by an unknown author: "Life is fragile; handle it with prayer." Black life is a life of fragility. Blacks are negatively affected by domestic violence, teenage pregnancy, school dropouts, jail and prison terms for young black males, substance abuse, AIDS, divorce, stress, poverty, unemployment, and underemployment. Black worship has helped persons hit by negativity to obtain help, hope, and healing. Preaching and worship have helped fractured families and individuals disabled by failure to experience the amazing grace of God that brings the victorious through many "dangers, toils, and snares."

As embracers of a trinitarian faith, we speak of God as Creator, Redeemer, and Sustainer. The God who created us redeemed us, and the God who redeemed us sustains us. Preaching and worship enable us to stay connected with God. Preaching and worship offer sanity to an insane world. In such a world where so much suffering is senseless, persons ask, "If the risen Christ is Lord, why do the good suffer?" In *Is God a White Racist?* W. R. Jones argues that God does not value all persons equally. He concludes that God is responsible for the imbalance of suffering that distinguishes the in group from the out group.[12]

Theologian Letty Russell argues that there is the Suffering God who has become one of us. Our ancestors did not debate issues of suffering and the justice of God. They were not "armchair philosophers of theodicy." They refused to blame God for their suffering. They also rejected suicide as an option. Their preaching and worship fueled their faith to proclaim:

> Done made my vow to the Lord,
> And I never will turn back,
> I will go, I shall go,
> To see what the end will be.[13]

From our sainted predecessors we have learned that through worship, we cultivate a personal relationship with God. Worship cleanses both the individual and the gathered community through the forgiveness of God and through the restoration and renewal of a proper relationship with God. Through worship, God's power regenerates and energizes the church to become like Christ in mood, manners, and mission.

Worship comes from the Anglo-Saxon word *weorthscipe*— *worth* and *ship*—which means "to give reverence and honor." The Hebrew word is *Kabod*, which means "the honor and weight of God." The New Testament word *doxa* means "God is worthy of honor." In the New Testament the word *proskunes* means "to kiss the hand toward one" or to "prostrate oneself" before another in worship. The English term *liturgy* has its roots in the Greek *leitourgia*, which means "ministry" or "service." All of these First Testament and Second Testament terms with Hebrew and Greek origins describe in part what true worship is. Professor

Franklin M. Segler states: "Christian worship defies definition; it can only be experienced."[14]

The pastor and the minister of music should work together with a music committee to carefully plan and organize each worship service. The sermon, the scriptures, the songs, and the litanies should harmonize to meet the particular theme of each worship service. Each service should begin with a call to worship, which will direct the congregation to focus their minds on God. The call to worship usually comes from a passage of scripture, a hymn, or an appropriate word. Sometimes the choir sings the call to worship. Then the processional of choir and clergy will begin. In the high church tradition, the bishop is to be the last person to march in. In the free church tradition, the senior pastor and a guest preacher (if there is a guest speaker) are the last to march from the narthex to the pulpit during the processional. Old and New Testament scriptures are usually read after the congregation stands and sings the hymn of praise. An invocation invites God to be accepting of the worshipers' presence. It should be brief because the pastoral prayer, which petitions God to be responsive to congregational needs, is a priestly prayer much longer in length, and it will be prayed prior to the delivery of the sermon. In African American churches the visitors are always welcomed.

There can be no worship without the presentation of gifts. In some churches there is a call for tithes and offerings. Great stress is placed on a stewardship litany, and people are made aware of the fact that giving is a part of Christian living. Some churches have a mission offering, which occurs early in the service. The later offering is to assist the church in meeting its operational budget.

Worshipful giving is an expression of gratitude to God for all of God's gifts, both material and spiritual. Worshipful giving is a tangible way to express our love for mission causes and for the world's needy. A prayer of thanksgiving for the money given is always in order. In Protestant services, the congregations of each denomination meet on stated times to observe baptismal services and the Lord's Supper. People wait with eager anticipation for the preached word. Good, well-prepared sermons touch the hearts of the hearers. The word-of-mouth presentations inspire new members to tell their friends and relatives. The evangelistic energy of new members helps all churches to grow numerically and spiritually. Holistic worship touches upon the totality of responsible Christian living.

Worship life in African American churches would improve greatly if church boards would budget more generously for paid staff persons who operate the taping media and church sound systems. Trustees often are blind to the importance of having high-quality sound equipment and musical instruments that help provide attractive worship services, which fill empty pews. Many a preacher with an excellent message has failed because the microphones were not working properly or the pulpit lights or the auditorium lights were inferior. Willie Eva Smith reminds us that "many of our churches could do better toward recompensing good musicians."[15]

The value that churches place on providing the best possible staff for worship leadership may indicate the poverty or richness of the lay leaders who control local church budgets and who oversee local church politics to the detriment or the advancement of the worship and outreach agendas of black churches. Many gifted and dedicated staff are either driven away from local church ministries or demoralized in these ministries because of the spiritual blindness of lay leaders who disrespect the vision of God-anointed pastors and church staff. Growing churches and churches with the potential to reach higher levels of effective ministries and transformational spiritual growth are the results of experiences of worshiping the Lord God in the beauty of holiness. Authentic preaching and worship change with changing times as led by the creativity of the Holy Spirit. May the churches of the twenty-first century hear and obey what the Holy Spirit is saying.

Earlier I endeavored to share with the reader my critical reflections on preaching and worship from a technical and theological perspective. Before concluding this work, I shall relate how relevant preaching and vibrant worship can promote church growth. In 1970 when I became the pastor of Allen Temple, the worship attendances in two services ranged from three hundred to three hundred fifty people. The church services were highly liturgical for an African American Baptist church. The pastor wore the liturgical stoles that were in keeping with the church season of the church year. The call and response rhythm to the singing and preaching were not present. No one was heard saying "Amen" to the sermon points articulated by the preaching. The worship was European in design and style. Drums were not welcome in the service. The masses did not visit

Allen Temple for Sunday morning worship. The saying in the community was that "Allen Temple is where the intellectual people worship. The sermon preached there is not a sermon. It is a lecture."

I had to change the image of Allen Temple. First of all, I connected with the people in the community by becoming a prophetic voice that advocated justice. I dressed in African robes and pushed a program of black consciousness. I became known for preaching with sense and soul. In my sermonic content there was meat to mentally digest, and there was soul or passion in sermonic delivery. The congregation was freed to talk back to me during the delivery of the sermon. People with doctors' degrees and no degrees responded to my giving an invitation after the sermon.

We outgrew our facilities and built a new sanctuary despite the protestations of the naysayers who said that the new people would not help pay the church's bills and that if we built the new church, it would never be full. Instead of debating with the naysayers we continued to love all of the people while developing excellent worship services and preaching sermons that met the needs of all age groups.

While emphasizing Christian education and stewardship in order to disciple the new people who were joining, we became strong enough financially to hire support staff. Mrs. Betty Gadling, a gifted composer and director, was hired to become our minister of music. Pastoral support staff was developed to provide a team ministry to allow me time to prepare strong sermons that meet the needs of diverse Sunday morning audiences. In order to keep the momentum of growth strong, preachers of national reputation and popularity are invited to preach for special days and for spiritual renewal events. The children and youth lead the second Sunday worship services. The young adults lead the third Sunday services. The men lead the fourth Sunday services. Allen Temple church growth takes preaching and music from the sanctuary to the street corners of East Oakland.

As the demographics changed, Allen Temple changed to embrace the Spanish-speaking community in Oakland. The Reverend Reuben Hurtado is the Spanish-speaking pastor in charge of the Spanish-speaking worship services. Annually, I preach in Spanish at the Spanish-speaking services.

Things do not remain the same; therefore, it is necessary to make adjustments in style and form in order to attract people from nonchurch backgrounds to our ever-changing and ever-growing church.

Notes

1. Teresa L. Fry Brown, *Weary Throats and New Songs: Black Women Proclaiming God's Word* (Nashville: Abingdon Press, 2003), 53.

2. Olin P. Moyd, *The Sacred Art: Preaching and Theology in the African American Tradition* (Valley Forge, Pa.: Judson Press, 1995), 10.

3. Henry H. Mitchell, *Black Preaching* (New York: J. B. Lippincott, 1970), 203.

4. Carlyle Fielding Stewart III, *Joy Songs, Trumpet Blasts, and Hallelujah Shouts* (Lima, Ohio: CSS Publishing Company, 1997), 13.

5. Ibid., 14.

6. Ibid., 16-19.

7. Ibid., 20-22.

8. Ibid., 130.

9. James A. Noel and Matthew V. Johnson, eds., *The Passion of the Lord: African American Reflections* (Minneapolis: Augsburg Fortress Press, 2005), 22.

10. Howard Thurman, *The Growing Edge* (Richmond, Ind.: Friends United Press, 1974), 33.

11. J. Alfred Smith Sr., *A Prayer Wheel Turning* (Morristown, N.J.: Aaron Press, 1989), 73.

12. William R. Jones, *Is God a White Racist? A Preamble to Black Theology* (Garden City, N.Y.: Anchor Press, 1973), 4.

13. Howard Thurman, *Deep River and the Negro Spiritual Speaks of Life and Death* (Richmond, Ind.: Friends United Press, 1975), 34.

14. Franklin M. Segler, *Christian Worship: Its Theology and Practice* (Nashville: Broadman Press, 1967), 6.

15. Willie Eva Smith, *O Sing Unto the Lord a New Song: A Complete Handbook for the Total Church Music Program* (New York: Vantage Press, 1976), 56.

CHAPTER FIVE

GROWING THE AFRICAN AMERICAN CHURCH THROUGH WORSHIP AND PREACHING

Jeremiah A. Wright Jr.

In December of 1961, the United Church of Christ launched its fourth African American congregation in the state of Illinois with a new church start on the South Side of Chicago. Back in the days when integration was the goal and desire of mainline denominations, the United Church of Christ's local bodies through the Chicago Metropolitan Association and the Illinois Conference of the United Church of Christ envisioned a "black and white together" congregation as they established their new church start right on the edges of an integrated (or desegregated) community.

Unfortunately as in most mainline denominations back in the early 1960s, the notion of integration meant that blacks should adopt a white lifestyle, a white way of worship, European values, and European American ways of viewing reality. That was who we were when we started, and that was how we saw ourselves!

For the first seven years of Trinity United Church of Christ's existence, the church grew slowly. The church planters and church planners selected a neighborhood in which new split-level homes for blacks were being built. As was the thinking for almost every new church start in a mainline denomination in those days, the church was designed to attract "our kind of people."

"Our kind of people" meant home-owning, upper-middle income, African American families and white families. The fashionable term for our congregation in the early 1960s was *middle-class* families.

In 1968, however, a major change took place across this nation in the African American community. In that year, Dr. Martin Luther King, Jr., was assassinated.

One of the black journalists in the city of Chicago, Lu Palmer (a graduate of Virginia Union University), coined a phrase that explains what happened in the nation when King was killed. His phrase also explains what happened in the African American community throughout the country and what happened in African American churches and mainline denominations. Mr. Palmer said, "It was enough to make a Negro turn Black!"

Prior to 1968 no authentic black music was allowed to be sung on black college campuses throughout the country. The "concretized" and "anthemically arranged" Negro spirituals were a part of every college choir's repertoire.

I was a soloist from 1959 through 1961 in the concert choir of Virginia Union University, and our concerts consisted of European anthems in the first half and arranged Negro spirituals in the second half. There was no singing of any other genres of black music allowed in the Virginia Union Concert Choir!

There was no meter singing (long meter, short meter, or common meter). There was no shape note singing, and there definitely was no gospel music allowed. The white missionaries had taught us at the black colleges that that kind of music was not sacred music and it was not worthy of "serious study."

In the worship services of mainline denominations, therefore, those of us who "knew better" understood that we did not sing what the lower classes sang. We did not sing what uneducated Negroes sang. We knew how to worship God "properly," and our worship services were often described as services that could "out-white white people's services."

Important Point

We sang hymns from the white hymnals. We sang anthems, and we sang *arranged* Negro spirituals. Our churches preferred pipe organs, but for a small congregation like Trinity, all we could afford was an Allen organ that sounded like a pipe organ.

There definitely were no Hammond B3s allowed in upwardly mobile, educated Negro congregations. There were no drums, no electric pianos, no tambourines, and no washboards. There were no shekeres and no percussive instruments that would dare remind any Negro of Africa or of non-European music!

Because the United Church of Christ (UCC) ordained only seminary graduates in the 1960s, our trained clergy's ways of conducting worship services, and especially of preaching, were to follow the European and European

American pattern to the letter. There was to be no emotion-
alism in the worship service.

The sermons were to be fine-tuned homilies that lasted
from fifteen to twenty minutes, and the worship service
was to be over within an hour. On Communion Sundays no
one minded if the service lasted an hour and ten minutes.

A pastor of one of our four black UCC congregations in
the 1960s had the audacity to say publicly from the pulpit,
"We will tolerate no 'niggerisms' in our services!" That
meant no one could shout. That meant there would be no
hand waving. That meant there would be no hand clapping. That meant there would be no displays of emotion
allowed in a Congregationalist church.

Unfortunately, Trinity United Church of Christ was made
from that same mold, and for seven years that is how the
worship services were at Trinity. In 1968, however, when
Negroes turned black, the church started to die. All across
the country, gospel music started being sung not only on
black college campuses but also in black "silk-stocking"
churches.

Gospel music was heard after 1968 in Roman Catholic
parishes, in Anglican churches, in United Methodist
churches, in Lutheran churches (ELCA), in American
Baptist churches, and in United Church of Christ churches.
Black gospel choirs were formed on all campuses—black
and white! One ironic footnote of history is that in 1974 at
the National Black Gospel Choir contest, the black gospel
choir from Northwestern University took first place.

Black college students began to say after 1968 that they
were not going to let the institutions of learning make them

worship as white people worshiped any longer. Students were not willing to give up their Africanity for their Christianity.

Students were not willing to buy into the notion that gospel music was for uneducated and lower-class blacks. Gospel music was our music, and gospel music was going to be sung by persons with PhDs, JDs, and every other kind of earned degree!

For the older members of mainline Negro congregations, however, that new attitude on the part of educated folk (who should have "known better") was anathema. Many of the older members, ministers, and musicians refused to allow that kind of "heathen" music in their churches, and as a result, their churches began to die. Trinity Church began to die also.

By the fall of 1971, our 500-plus-member church had dwindled down to 87 adult members, and the congregation decided that it had to change. Members of the congregation asked a very painful question: "Are we going to be a black church in the black community, related to and relevant for the black community, or are we going to continue to be a white church in blackface?"

Dr. Reuben Sheares (my immediate predecessor, the interim pastor of our church from the fall of 1971 until February of 1972) said that the question our congregation had to ask was a very painful one. It was a question that caused members to come to grips with some very painful decisions that they had made about turning their backs on their own culture, turning their backs on their own people, turning their backs on their own heritage, and turning their backs on their own relatives!

As Dr. Sheares told me one day, "Many black people joined a white church to get away from black people, Jerry! When they joined a white denomination, they did not want to hear any more gospel—sung or preached!"

The adult members of Trinity Church in 1971, however, made a decision to be a black church. They made a decision to change the way they related to the community. At that time our church offered only one class to the community—and it was a yoga class!

There was no Bible study. There were no programs that related to the community. The worship service definitely was not attractive to black people, and the church was viewed as the "Negro church" that sat in the middle of a black community!

The search committee of the congregation put together a vision statement of what they wanted to become as a black church in the black community. They showed that vision statement to everyone who was a candidate for the pulpit of Trinity, and they asked the candidates, "Can you lead us in this direction?" When they asked me that question, I responded, "It would be like throwing Brer Rabbit into the briar patch!"

I made that statement because I had been at Howard University when Negroes turned black. In 1968, the music majors at Howard University "turned the ships around." They closed down the Fine Arts Building and said to the director of the famed Howard University Concert Choir that there would not be any more music taught in that building until black music was brought into it.

In a public debate waged on the steps of the Fine Arts Building (after they had closed it down), they said to the choir director that they were tired of singing German lieder and Italian arias to prove that they were intelligent. They wanted to sing their own music.

They reasoned that it was insane for them to be at a black school and not be able to take courses in African music (West African, East African, and southern African music), Caribbean music, Brazilian music, Cuban music, blues, jazz, and gospel music! They thought it was the height of insult to have jazz artists such as Duke Ellington and Count Basie being given honorary degrees by white schools while they attended a black school that offered no courses in which they could learn the jazz that the white schools were honoring!

They argued that the blues was created by black people, but there were no courses on the blues at Howard University. They argued that gospel music was created by Thomas Dorsey, but there were no courses on gospel music.

The conductor of the Howard University Concert Choir said to them, "But that is folk music—unworthy of serious study!" They asked him if folk music was not worthy of serious study, why did he have them learning Russian folk songs?

The answer was obvious. The answer was that Russia was in Europe, and European music from classical to contemporary was worthy of serious study. Only black music was not worthy of serious study. They said to him in no uncertain terms that those days were over and that they were going to have some black music taught in their school or there would be no more Music Department at Howard University.

They immediately formed the Howard University Gospel Choir and marched into Rankin Chapel with tambourines and drums, and college and graduate students began shouting and dancing with joy to be able to sing their own music and affirm their own history, heritage, and culture. The director of the famed Howard University Concert Choir had a heart attack!

Many musicians in mainline denomination black congregations also had apoplexy when the graduates of schools like Howard demanded gospel music beginning back in 1968. They, too, had been taught that that was not sacred music.

Having seen the formation of the Howard University Gospel Choir, having been there when it started, having heard the rationale, and having experienced educated blacks desiring their own music, I knew what the members of Trinity meant when they asked to go in a new direction and become a black church in the black community.

My first change as the pastor of Trinity and the worship leader was to add some black hymns. The United Church of Christ hymnal (back then it was the Congregational Church's hymnal) did not have simple or traditional hymns like "What a Fellowship," "At the Cross," "Nothing but the Blood," and "Jesus, Keep Me Near the Cross."

I knew that if we were going to attract members of the black community, we needed black music. So, I started picking the hymn of the day each Sunday on my first Sunday as pastor in March of 1972. I made it a hymn that black people knew out of their own tradition. I also instituted an altar call (a prayer where worshipers are called to come and kneel at the altar beneath the old rugged cross), and I instituted the hymn of invitation.

To the average reader, that last sentence seems incredible! Many people cannot conceive of a black worship service without a hymn of invitation and an invitation for worshipers to come to Christ.

Our church, which was started by a white denomination (please remember), did not have a hymn of invitation. We had a notice in the bulletin that announced, "If you are interested in uniting with this congregation, please fill out the card that you will find on the back of the pew. Drop it in the offering plate, and the deacons of the church will come and visit you."

Just adding those three new songs changed the texture of our Sunday worship services. We have never been the same!

In 1972, our Allen organ was not capable of producing the sound that African American urban dwellers are used to in black worship services, so within a few years after my arrival we purchased a Hammond B3 that would give us the gospel sound we needed. That instrument, along with the formation of the Trinity Choral Ensemble, which sang all genres of music—including contemporary gospel music—started to attract visitors and new members by the dozens.

W. E. B. DuBois said in 1903 that there are three ingredients to any black church that is a black church in this country. The three ingredients are preaching, music, and the Holy Spirit. (DuBois with his Harvard-educated mind-set called the Holy Spirit "frenzy"! What he meant as a pejorative term, however, is a descriptive term.) When the preaching and the music are from the heart, the Holy Spirit will come into a worship service, and it is the combination of those three that causes a church to grow. It is definitely what caused our church to grow.

I was reared in the black church tradition on the East Coast of the country. I grew up around clergypersons who had been to seminary. Because I was born in 1941, most of the pastors I met had attended one of the three black seminaries. There were only three accredited black seminaries in the 1940s and 1950s (Virginia Union University, Howard University, and what is now called the Interdenominational Theological Seminary in Atlanta).

I was used to hearing educated preachers who still had "soul." Their sermons were not all "heady." Their sermons were what Howard Thurman calls a combination of "head and heart." I understood that to be the genius of black preaching, and I also understood that to be the only way I could preach.

One of our members, an appellate court judge, Justice R. Eugene Pincham, says, "You can't be what you can't see!" All I had seen was trained clergy who did not give up the black style of preaching because of the substantive things they had learned in seminary.

That was how my father preached. That was how my mother preached. That is how my uncle, John B. Henderson, preached, and that is how my grandfather, Hamilton Martin Henderson, preached.

I brought that history and that heritage of preaching to the pulpit of Trinity United Church of Christ, and the change in preaching style and the change in music style in our worship services have caused our church to grow from 87 adult members to 8,500 active members today!

I used to tease Lyle Schaller (America's guru on church growth) about my not having ever read any of his books. I told Dr. Schaller that I did not need to read his books because the second chapter of Acts was my manual on church growth.

In the second chapter of Acts, Luke says that more than three thousand people joined the church on one day because of what happened in worship. The people *saw* something. The people *heard* something. The people *felt* something, and they were convicted in their hearts about Christ. People joined the church in Luke's day because of worship, and people joined Trinity United Church of Christ from 1972 until this present day because of worship.

When my minister of music, who served along with me for thirty years, was in his early years as my partner in leading worship, he used to complain to me and say that I wanted perfection. I clarified his complaint by saying to him that I did not want *perfection* in my Music Department. I wanted *excellence*!

I wanted every choir in our church to perform excellently at every worship service. In fact, I told him that I did not want *performance*; I wanted *ministry*! We have three services every Sunday, and I did not want worshipers picking and choosing the service they would attend based upon the music they would hear. I wanted them to hear excellent anthems, excellent spirituals, excellent hymns, excellent meter singing, and excellent gospel music no matter what service they attended on any given Sunday.

He and I learned the hard way why having two different styles of singing can split a congregation right down the middle. When the Trinity Choral Ensemble was started, it had a drawing power that was almost indescribable.

The Trinity Choral Ensemble came into being because of the young people of our church. In July of 1972 (I started in March of 1972), the president of our youth fellowship said to me, "Rev, we want a choir for the young folk!" I said to him, "You have the Children's Choir (our Little Warriors for Christ)." He said that he meant a choir for the teenagers.

I told him to hook up with the church's director of music, rehearse a few times, and then let me know when he thought they would be ready to sing for a Sunday morning worship service. In September of 1972, he called me late one night after their choir rehearsal, complaining that the choir director had them singing European songs. He said they wanted to sing black gospel music.

When I asked him if he had shared his desire with the director of music, he said, "Yes, but she said that she could not play that kind of music or teach that kind of music." She had been taught at one of our black colleges that black gospel music was not sacred music!

Then I asked him if he knew anybody who could play and teach black gospel music as well as the anthems, the spirituals, and the hymns. He told me about a nineteen-year-old college student who lived three doors from the old church parsonage and who was a freshman in college majoring in music.

I warned the president of the youth fellowship that we did not have much money. We had only a $39,000 annual budget! I told him that as a young person who was born and raised in the United Church of Christ, he should take another teenager who was also born in our denomination and go to the Executive Council of the church and request some dollars to pay this young man. The Executive Council gave our youth $150 for the balance of the year to pay for the teenage musician.

They rehearsed for one month, and the president called me excited, asking me to come and hear them. I did and I was deeply impressed! I let them sing on the fifth Sunday in October of 1972.

They made their debut as the Youth Fellowship Choir of Trinity United Church of Christ. They came in "stepping" like members of Omega Psi Phi or Delta Sigma Theta at a step show. They wore red and green dashikis with black trousers or black miniskirts that Sunday.

They had drums, tambourines, and one washboard, and the nature of our worship at Trinity United Church of Christ was changed forever. Most of the adults who complained to me were not complaining about the noise level, the drums, the steps, the swaying, the tambourines, or the washboard. They complained because the choir was called the "Youth Fellowship Choir of Trinity United Church of Christ," and as adults, they wanted to get in that choir!

The following year, we changed the name of the choir to the Trinity Choral Ensemble, and we opened the membership to persons of all ages. That choir soon had several sets of parents and children singing in the same group, and the choral members spilled out of the choir loft into the first few pews of the sanctuary. Every Sunday that they sang there would be standing room only in our congregation.

When the Chancel Choir of the church sang, however, old members, new members, visitors, and lovers of gospel music would not come! Please remember: the Trinity Choral Ensemble sang anthems, hymns, spirituals, *and* gospel music.

The Chancel Choir did not sing gospel. What soon happened was that we had two different congregations. The few folk who liked "the old way" would come when the Chancel Choir would sing. But, the church would be jam-packed when the Trinity Choral Ensemble would sing.

After five years of limping along like that, I called a meeting and asked my "teenage" musician (who was then twenty-four years old) to bring the presidents and the section leaders of both choirs together for the meeting. I explained to them that we were combining the choirs and that we would have one adult choir in the church.

That one adult choir would be called the Sanctuary Choir of Trinity United Church of Christ. It would sing fifty-two Sundays a year, and it would sing all genres of music. My musician, Jeffrey Radford, was very nervous. He knew that members of the Chancel Choir did not like to sway. They did not like drums. They did not like gospel music. He realized that merging those two choirs would cause many of them to leave the choir.

I told Mr. Radford that if he would stick to the vision, God would send voices that would help us realize that vision. I was right. The Sanctuary Choir today has more than 250 voices in it!

Because of the church growth, we had to build a new worship center. The sanctuary in which we were worshiping in 1972 held 200 people.

The Trinity Choral Ensemble had more than 80 voices in it by its second year. We constructed a 600-seat sanctuary that would accommodate 900 with chairs down, and by using the overflow, that sanctuary (so we thought) would accommodate our phenomenal growth. On the first Sunday that we marched into our new sanctuary, however, we had chairs down, and we had worshipers standing in the aisles and along the wall! We expanded to two services a Sunday to try to accommodate the growth.

We constructed the new sanctuary in 1978, and by 1980, we were doing three services every Sunday. We still had worshipers standing along the wall, so we went to a fourth service, which was a Saturday night service, by the mid-1980s.

Again and again, our members told us that the worship service drew them to the church. DuBois was right. The preaching and the music ushered in the Holy Spirit, and the Holy Spirit drew thousands of members to our congregation!

In 1988, the unbelievable crowding in the sanctuary (and the physical toll that four services a weekend were taking on my body) eventuated in the congregation voting to construct a third worship center. We built a 2,700-seat sanctuary, and we still have worshipers in two overflow rooms on Sundays.

Because of our multiple services, we had to provide some relief for the Sanctuary Choir, so we formed two other major singing groups. We changed the Men's Chorus and the Women's Chorus from being choirs that sang only on Men's Day and Women's Day to choirs that sang several times each month. And the Women's Chorus now has more than 200 voices while the Men's has 110 voices.

The Sanctuary Choir is heard every Sunday, but we rotate the other choirs into the singing calendar as follows: on the first Sunday, the Sanctuary Choir sings the first two services, and the Women's Chorus sings at the 6:00 p.m. service. Yes! With a sanctuary that seats 2,700, we still need three services on a Sunday!

On the second Sunday, our Elementary School Choir and our Teenage Choir sing at the first service, and the Sanctuary Choir sings at the 11:00 a.m. and the 6:00 p.m. services. On the third Sunday, our Women's Chorus sings at the first service. The Sanctuary Choir sings at 11:00 a.m., and the Men's Chorus sings at the 6:00 p.m. service. On the fourth Sunday, our Men's Chorus sings at the early service. The Sanctuary Choir sings at 11:00 a.m., and the Women's Chorus sings at the 6:00 p.m. service.

I spend a great deal of my time each week preparing the worship services. I have to get my selected songs and my scripture and sermon title to the musicians in time for their rehearsals so that the worship experience becomes a "total package" with the ministry of music and the ministry of the spoken word inextricably bound one to another.

As the worship leader and the one designing worship each week, I pick the morning hymn and the songs leading into and following my sermon. That makes music an integral part of the worship experience. That makes worship the "glue" that holds the service together, undergirds the sermon, and enables the worshiper to experience the presence of God in a deep and personal way.

Because preaching is one of the three ingredients that DuBois called a sine qua non, I not only try to model excellence in preaching but also try to bring before our congregation the most excellent preachers in the nation.

Because I want my seminarians to see the importance of academic training, I have brought and will continue to bring the most highly qualified persons, academically and spiritually, whom it has been my pleasure to hear and to know. The congregation of Trinity Church has heard preachers such as Dr. Gardner C. Taylor, Dr. Samuel DeWitt Proctor, Dr. Wyatt T. Walker, Dr. Harold Carter, Dr. Michael Eric Dyson, Dr. Frederick G. Sampson, Dr. Anthony C. Campbell, Rev. Roscoe D. Cooper, Dr. Charles G. Adams, and Dr. D. E. King. The preaching of Dr. James A. Forbes, Father Michael Pfleger, Rev. Troy Bonner, Dr. William Curtis, Dr. Marcus Cosby, Rev. Otis Moss III, Dr. Rudolph McKissick Jr., and Dr. Frederick Douglas Haynes III has enriched our congregation.

Our members have heard Dr. Alison Gise Johnson, Bishop Vashti McKenzie, Dr. Ann Lightner, Dr. Cynthia Hale, Dr. Claudette Copeland, Rev. Iyanla Vanzant, Dr. Debra Grant, Dr. Prathia Hall, and Dr. Renita Weems. The preaching of Dr. Johnny Ray Youngblood, Dr. James Perkins, Dr. Arthur T. Jones, Dr. Earl B. Mason, Bishop Nathaniel Jarrett, Rev. Dennis Proctor, Dr. Jessica Ingram, Dr. Frank Thomas, Rev. Alvin O'Neal Jackson, Rev. Robert M. Burkins, Dr. Jerry Cannon, and Rev. Sean McMillan has blessed them.

Beginning with that first service back on the fifth Sunday of October of 1972 when I let our teenagers sing, I have programmed four Youth Sundays a year. These services usually are held during months when there are five Sundays. The young people lead our worship service from the call to worship down to the benediction. They also bring the morning message.

For the first twenty years of my pastorate, I went over the preaching of the morning message with the young person who was scheduled to speak that day. I wanted to impress (and still want to impress!) upon our young people the importance of the preached word. I want them to have content that is sound, and I want them to combine "head and heart" in the same way that every preacher they hear at their church does.

Over the past decade or so, the youth minister on our staff has taken on that responsibility for me, and he now goes over the teenagers' sermons with them to make sure that the preached moment is a powerful moment in the worship experience for those who gather at Trinity United Church of Christ.

I have a passion for worship. I believe that worship not only helps the church to grow but also helps make sense of the world in which we live.

The songs provide a lift for our souls and our spirits. The sermons must provide the word of God for the people of God, and the sermons have to tie the world in which we live to the Living Word that God sent unto this world.

I often joke with one of my sons in the ministry by saying, "Thank God for Sunday!" If it were not for Sunday and for the worship hour, there would be no way that we could make it through the week. I thank God for the way God has honored our efforts to be faithful to him in worship, and I thank God for the privilege of serving God's people by offering my best to him who offered his life!

PART THREE

Outreach

CHAPTER SIX

CHURCH GROWTH THROUGH COMMUNITY OUTREACH

A MINISTRY OF COMMUNITY REDEMPTION

James C. Perkins

The idea of church growth is usually associated with the dynamics of suburban church life. Mention the topic of church growth in a casual conversation with many pastors and laypersons, and more times than not the name of the pastor of some large suburban church will surface.

Many pastors and congregations located in the inner cities look at their suburban counterparts and are tempted to be envious. Large, sprawling campuses, big parking lots, and comfortable building facilities to provide space for all the ministry needs are any pastor's dream. Inner-city pastors know, however, that their ministry context will never be a carbon copy of their suburban church counterparts. The very nature of inner-city life demands a different kind of ministry. By any gauge, ministry is hard work. But the nature of life in the inner city requires a congregation to have the will to take creative steps to address a wide range of problems with which churches in small towns and suburban communities do not have to contend, at least to the same extent.

Poverty, poor housing, unemployment, drugs, and crime are grim realities that touch the lives of people whether they live in a suburban or inner-city setting, but these and other related social problems are vastly more pronounced in urban life and require that a church focus on one or several of these issues as an outreach focus in order for that ministry to grow.

People do not necessarily attend a church just because it is located in their neighborhood. People shop for churches just as they shop for clothes or other items. They are looking for a church with a ministry that meets their needs spiritually, physically, and socially.

Suburban life used to be thought of as the exclusive privilege of the white middle class who left the inner cities during the 1950s and 1960s. But the 'burbs are no longer the domain of whites. Many middle-class African American families have also left the inner city to escape the problems of urban life, to rear their families in more serene surroundings, to send their children to better schools, and perhaps to live closer to their places of employment.

When I came to Detroit in 1981, Motown was the fourth largest city in the United States. More than twenty years later, it has slipped from the top ten cities list to number eleven. This is not just the result of white flight. For a number of reasons, suburban life is attractive to African Americans as well.

Church growth is not just a white church suburban experience. Many growing African American churches are suburban churches too. Bishop Eddie Long, Creflo Dollar, and Bishop T. D. Jakes, to name a few of the obvious ones, are founding pastors of large ministries located in the suburbs of Atlanta and Dallas, respectively.

As alluring and desirable as it may be, all pastors cannot leave the inner city and relocate to the suburbs. Some of us have discovered that we are called to stay and serve where God has placed us, and if we are faithful, our churches can grow too.

From Illusion to Reality

I assumed my pastoral responsibilities at the Greater Christ Baptist Church, Detroit, Michigan, on the first Sunday in January 1981. As a young, ambitious minister in a large city, I thought that church growth involved strong preaching. I thought that if I just preached hard enough on a consistent basis, it would generate church growth.

To be sure, preaching is a key ingredient in church growth, but it is not the only factor. As I found out, preaching without a strong support system of meaningful, relevant ministry will leave preacher and people feeling empty and disconnected from real-life situations. Church growth preaching must not simply be a display of eloquence and erudition. It must speak to real-life issues with supporting ministries that concretize the preaching in the lives of the people. In short, the Word must become flesh and dwell among us (John 1:14).

Spiritual Preparation

This fact came home to me clearly after several years of ministry at the Greater Christ Baptist Church. The weekly worship experience was fine. A few people attended the weekly prayer service and Bible study, but I was restless in my spirit because we weren't experiencing either the spiritual or the numerical growth that I thought was possible.

The first thing I had to do—and which I recommend to any pastor who wants his or her church to grow—was to pray. As simplistic as it may sound, the spiritual preparation of the pastor and the people is key to spiritual transformation, both personal and corporate.

The power of prayer in the life of the pastor and the people of God cannot be overstated. Jesus told his disciples to "pray ... the Lord of the harvest, that he will send forth labourers into his harvest" (Matthew 9:38 KJV). The vision for one's ministry emerges from one's prayer life, and prayer clarifies it. Prayer is a way to transcend the barriers and blockades that prohibit growth. Ministry is not accomplished just by having good sense and a good education. Ministry emerges out of a brooding and mourning spirit over the condition of the people.

Nehemiah began his great work of rebuilding the wall around Jerusalem through the spiritual discipline of praying and mourning for his people (Nehemiah 1:4-11). Out of the prayer and mourning experience developed what I call a vision of community redemption. Simply stated, it means that saved people have a responsibility to turn around and save their surroundings. Like Nehemiah, every urban pastor knows that if his or her church is going to grow, he or she will have to initiate a ministry that reaches out to the surrounding community and engages in the task of rebuilding.

This perspective is the result of engaging in prayer over the condition of one's surroundings. Shawchuck and Heuser state: "Vision never comes in a vacuum; it comes in response to a real call and is germane to a specific time and place.... A vision aligns one's thinking and feeling and doing into one common volition, in which one would rather die than not try."[1]

Growth—A By-product of Service

Even after a vision for my ministry began to be born in me, my motivation was not growth, that is, not in the numerical sense. My motivation was to serve. Like Nehemiah, I saw people in dire straits. They were unemployed. They were drug addicted. They had no relationship with the organized church, except to show up to beg for food or clothes. These realities made me feel uneasy and irresponsible in my business-as-usual approach to ministry. My seminary education prepared me to preach sermons, but not to meet the real life-and-death needs of a people. Through prayer, God spoke to me and led me to another level of service.

Growth occurs when we engage in a ministry that meets the real needs of people.

Restructuring the Church

The congregation must also be prepared to envision a ministry for the community. A pastor with a vision to which the congregation is not connected will only frustrate the pastor and the people.

Too many congregations are so tied to their traditions and the practices they have carried on for years that they have isolated themselves from reality and insulated themselves from change. A pastor cannot assume that the people are going to follow him or her in the process of reorganizing the church for a new kind of ministry. He or she has to carry the people along with him or her.

One has to announce to the congregation that God wants the members to build a ministry that meets the real needs of the surrounding community as opposed to just meeting the personal ego needs of a few people who have been members of that congregation for a while.

He or she has to invite the people to engage in the spiritual preparation for a new vision. Bible studies that focus on the mission of the church must be initiated. Ministry leaders must be approached one by one and engaged in a dialogue about the church's need to reach out to the surrounding community. Sermons become more meaningful because they proclaim the coming of the Lord to that local situation.

Restructuring has to be done. New ministry groups have to be formed around a real need. For example, there may be people in the congregation who are interested in helping older adults. Those people who have such an interest can be organized into a ministry group and encouraged to find out where these adults are in the surrounding community, what their needs are, and what they can do to meet those needs. One need could be as simple as providing them with transportation to the church. The church vans become true mediums of ministry, not just the private taxi service for a few club members. People are added to the worship service. Weekday activities planned for older adults at the church make the church meaningful during the week. Soon the church begins to become the focal point for those adults, who in turn tell their friends, who also begin to participate.

From Vision to Reality

In the mid-1980s I was leaving my church one day, only to be informed that a young girl had been raped in an abandoned building directly across the street. I didn't know the girl or her family, but I did feel that as a pastor in the community, and especially in such close proximity to that occurrence, I had to do something to change the situation so that nothing like that would ever happen near the church again.

Like Nehemiah, I saw that the walls had fallen down. The area where I was to minister was the site where the 1960s riots had broken out, and nothing had been done since that time to rebuild the community. Though I had been praying about what to do, this event propelled me into action.

I saw this as spiritual warfare. In that abandoned building, I saw in the Spirit how the devil will completely destroy a life and, ultimately, an entire people. I saw that our response as people of God to the blight and abandonment was to reclaim the areas and return them to constructive, productive use in the name of our Christ and his Kingdom.

I met with my officers and told them we had to buy that building. Though some questioned why we should and they didn't particularly see the necessity of the purchase, in the end they agreed to do it. We ended up putting a Burger King franchise on that site.

Doing this removed an eyesore from the community, created jobs for some people who had no employment, and generated another revenue stream for the church. It gave the church members a feeling of accomplishment in their desire to serve Christ by meeting real needs. And more important, new people started coming to the church because they had the sense that here was a church earnestly trying to do something in the community as opposed to staying cloistered behind sacred walls.

In order to experience growth, a church must constantly be reminded that Jesus' command to us was to "go into all the world" (Mark 16:15).

All too often we think of "the world" as Africa, India, the Philippines, or some distant land. In an urban setting, churches must see and know that "the world" begins when they open their doors. Urban centers are the most neglected mission fields in the world.

Develop a Plan of Outreach

Before Nehemiah began the actual work of rebuilding the wall, he did his homework so he would have a comprehensive understanding of the scope of the task before him.

make a clear plan for the community.

In like manner, we saw that to redeem a community, we would need a clear understanding of the nature and needs of the community. To accomplish this task, we partnered with the Urban Planning Department of Michigan State University. The department used our community as a classroom for the students and assisted us in creating a neighborhood development plan.

This plan included demographics related to social development, land use and zoning, community facilities and services, housing development, and economic development. These various reports highlighted the needs of the surrounding community and gave the church an opportunity to identify specific needs we would seek to meet as a focus of ministry.

Because children and youth were primarily underserved, unparented, and unchurched, we set out to develop a strong youth ministry. Bringing children and youth into the church eventually brings their parent(s) or caregiver(s). This provides the church an opportunity to develop ministries for children and youth as well as new ministries for the primary adults in their lives.

Here are examples of such ministries:

Family Counseling Center. Trained social workers and counselors provide parenting classes, conflict resolution classes, drug/alcohol counseling, and individual counseling.

Clients become members of the church. Members of the church become clients of the counseling center.

Federal Credit Union. Organizing this ministry assists families and individuals in the area of their finances. This ministry addresses personal and family budgets, highlights the importance of good credit, sets forth steps to establish credit, illustrates how to save to purchase a house, and explains other financial issues.

Individuals also give more to support the cost of the church's ministry.

Single Family Housing. To accomplish this ministry, the church has to create a separate 501(c)(3) entity comprised of its own board to oversee its operations. Engaging the services of a housing consultant, this organization can learn how to apply to develop housing in the community. People who become residents of this housing should know that this is the work of the church. Over time, many of them also become members of the church.

The Benjamin E. Mays Male Academy. This school was created to address the educational, social, and spiritual needs of young urban males. Beginning with students in kindergarten through grade three, the school has grown to include students through grade seven.

Unfortunately, young urban males drop out of school at an alarming rate. By the time they reach the fourth grade, they begin to skip school and have encounters with law enforcement officials that indicate they are on their way to a life of crime, time in prison, or a premature death.

Many urban mothers are looking for help to save their sons. This school became another avenue to lead young families into the church.

These are a few examples of the kinds of outreach ministries that can be created in an urban setting that will generate tremendous growth for a church.

In a ministry of community redemption, a church must identify its redemptive turf (the specific geographical area it intends to serve), discover the needs of the area, decide which specific need(s) it will create a ministry to address, and go for it. Meeting real needs along with the spiritual needs of people is a gospel imperative. In Matthew 25:35, Jesus said that those who inherited the kingdom of God were those who had met the real needs of people: "I was an hungred, and ye gave me meat: I was thirsty, and ye gave me drink: I was a stranger, and ye took me in" (KJV).

James wrote, "If a brother or sister be naked, and destitute of daily food, and one of you say unto them, Depart in peace, be ye warmed and filled; notwithstanding ye give them not those things which are needful to the body; what doth it profit?" (James 2:15-16 KJV).

Urban life is often hard and without the necessary support systems to develop and sustain it, many people get destroyed. An urban church that desires to grow can develop an outreach ministry that meets the physical, social, and spiritual needs of the people within its redemptive turf.

Stay Focused on the Mission of the Church

Having said this, I want readers to understand that outreach is just that. It is reaching out to bring those outside into the fellowship of the church. Once inside, these persons have to be disciplined. A new infrastructure of the church has to be organized to teach people how to live a Christ-centered life. Without keeping this focus on the mission of the church to make disciples, the church becomes just a social welfare agency. This isn't necessarily a bad thing, but it is not the mission of the church. Outreach ministry is a means to an end and not an end within itself. In order to be a spiritually healthy church, there must be balance between the outreach ministries and the inner life of the church. Those who are in the church must see outreach as a means of carrying out the mission of the church. Those who come into the church through the outreach ministries must see that the end is to become like Christ.

Summary

In the age of the megachurch movement, pastors of urban churches can revitalize and grow their ministries through creative outreach ministry to their surrounding community. There is no single way to accomplish outreach ministry. Through a congregation's prayerful, sincere desire to serve the people of God, God will reveal a vision that will guide his people into accomplishing the mission of community redemption.

Note

1. Norman Shawchuck and Roger Heuser, *Leading the Congregation: Caring for Yourself While Serving Others* (Nashville: Abingdon Press, 1993), 72.

CHAPTER SEVEN

CHURCH GROWTH THROUGH BACK-DOOR MINISTRY

Les Mangum

The idea of Back-Door Ministries is rooted in the approach that Jesus took to develop his ministry. During the first century A.D. the synagogue and the temple resembled the traditional church of today. There were many instances when Jesus taught and healed at both locations. The Pharisees, Sadducees, and other religious leaders often greeted Jesus' efforts to develop his ministries with resentment and challenges. The resulting conflicts would not support an environment in which Jesus could teach his disciples to share the good news that the salvation of the world had come. Hence, Jesus left the traditional locations of religious teaching and went out into the highways and byways of Israel to call his disciples.

Back-Door Ministries are an approach to reaching out today to people who would be less likely to come into the "front door" of many traditional churches. The hope of the Back-Door Ministry is to create an environment where people, who may feel uncomfortable in a traditional church setting, can hear the good news interpreted to them in ways that they understand. It should be an environment where people can raise issues and concerns about the religiosity of the church. Some people have avoided the traditional church because they wrongly perceived the church as a place only for saints, not sinners. Such a perception would naturally cause persons who have fallen into sin and vice to shy away. The Back-Door Ministry environment is one in which the leaders of a traditional church can interact with people who may have false perceptions of the church. This approach helps convert impediments into stepping-stones by winning the hearts and minds of those who may have felt left out.

Growth of Jesus' Ministry Begins with a Back-Door Approach

> As he walked by the Sea of Galilee, he saw two brothers, Simon, who is called Peter, and Andrew his brother, casting a net into the sea—for they were fishermen. And he said to them, "Follow me, and I will make you fish for people." Immediately they left their nets and followed him. As he went from there, he saw two other brothers, James son of Zebedee and his brother John, in the boat with their father Zebedee, mending their nets, and he called them. Immediately they left the boat and their father, and followed him. (Matthew 4:18-22)

Jesus called Simon Peter and his brother Andrew, along with James and John, the sons of Zebedee, from their vocations as fishermen. When they heard the call of Jesus, they left their nets and followed him. The craft of fishing had been the basis of their survival. Their parents trained them to cast their nets into the sea to catch fish, the sustenance of their lives. They were tried and tested by unpredictable storms on the Sea of Galilee. They learned to persist against the adversity of the sea to draw on its resources. They responded to the call of Jesus by leaving their vocations and following him, as symbolized by leaving their nets behind.

These four disciples went with Christ in anticipation of discovering a new vocation. They left the trade of their fathers to follow Jesus in eager expectation that they might find satisfaction for their young, restless spirits, which rose far beyond the limitations of human endeavors. Undoubtedly, Jesus had awakened the hidden desire within them to do more than satisfy the need for physical sustenance. They went with Jesus seeking to satisfy the indomitable curiosity of their minds, to learn the true meaning of life, to renew their spirits, and to find peace for their souls. These four disciples left fishing with little awareness that their vocation symbolized the intent of Jesus' ministry. They were the "first fish" drawn by Jesus to be taught to fish for others in need of salvation.

I believe that Christ continues to call disciples into a personal relationship with God through him—a personal relationship enriched, unfolded, and understood through reaching out to the community. Christ's call to these four disciples to become fishers of people is the same call to all who leave their way of living behind to follow Jesus. Through following Jesus, they would discover a new life of joy, peace, commitment, and purpose.

We have all left many different walks of life to walk with Jesus. All of us must be like those called before us and anticipate learning to become fishers of people through ministries of community outreach according to the needs and circumstances of our communities.

The Design and Structure of a Back-Door Ministry

I have identified five essential components of a Back-Door Ministry that are present in Jesus' approach to ministry.

1. Jesus called his disciples. The ministerial staff—church leaders assigned to this area of ministry—must actively recruit people to enter the programs that have been set up to give them a hand up into the church. The Back-Door Ministry approach is not discriminatory. People of all races and economic categories have issues with the traditional church that make them more suitable to be approached in a nontraditional way.

2. Jesus taught them who they were and what they were to become. Many candidates for the Back-Door Ministry—persons addicted to alcohol or drugs and other people of low self-esteem and ambition—have been marginalized by society. Jesus taught that you are "the salt of the earth" and "the light of the world" (Matthew 5:13-14). This was an extremely high compliment to pay people who thought little of themselves. We have to communicate the greatness that they have within them by looking at them not for what they have been but for what they can become through Christ.

3. Jesus ate and fellowshiped among sinners in the general community and took his disciples with him to demonstrate his love and compassion for all people.

4. He demonstrated how to reach out to people through responding to their needs by healing, offering salvation, and empowering them by connecting them to the spirit of God. Jesus' objective was to have the learner or disciple take over the role as teacher and leader. Many people who join the church through the back door have the potential of advancing the church's knowledge of reaching new generations of people with the gospel.

5. Jesus sent the disciples into the community to duplicate and extend his ministries unto the ends of the earth, causing the community to grow.

Integrating the Design and Structure of the Back-Door Ministry with the Concept of Becoming Fishers of People

The concept of becoming fishers of people as a result of Christ-centered teaching and training is vital to the Back-Door Ministry approach. Jesus points to catching "fish," or people, as the most important objective of the ministry. The "nets" symbolize the methods (programs) we use to help bring someone to Christ. The Back-Door Ministry in itself is a net, but there should be other nets within the net. The other nets, or programs, depend upon the kinds of people you are trying to reach and ultimately bring to Christ. Programs will never be sufficient in themselves; they are only tools. The traditional church must provide passionate people from its own ranks to develop these ministries by loving the people and interacting with them one on one. There is no substitute for human love and expression that are unleashed when we hug and embrace each other as equals in the sight of God.

The challenge faced by many churches today, particularly those planted in the inner cities of our country, is the continuance of teaching and training of church members and leaders from both a theological and christological perspective. By christological, I mean observing, studying, and practicing community outreach in ways that are consistent with narratives of Jesus in the New Testament. There are numerous dramatic illustrations, didactic teachings, and instructions that show us what it means to reach out to people in the community to address both material and spiritual needs.

The following is a true story of how I was saved through the Back-Door Ministries of The United Methodist Church. The narrative is titled "The Story of Two Fishermen (Ministries): The First Was Caught Up in Prayer and the Second Was Prepared to Catch Fish."

The First Fisherman

I went into a six-story walk-up on my block. I scurried to the back of the hallway where I stooped beneath a flight of steps on the ground floor. I perched on one knee and poured three bags of heroin into a tablespoon with an ounce of water. I heated the spoon over the flame of two matches. I drew the clear substance through the hypodermic needle into a syringe. I hobbled farther beneath the steps to conceal myself from anyone who might walk in the building. I pressed my back against the wall and steadied myself. I injected the bulging blue vein in the pit of my arm, between my fist rotating and pumping wildly on one end and a belt drawn tightly around my biceps, cutting off circulation, on the other. An unbroken stream of blood rose slowly to the top of the clear tube and mushroomed. Before the drug had any effect on me, I felt a sustained, disturbing vibration in my body, and I heard deep bass and high-pitched sounds. They were coming through the wall I was leaning against. My body began to shake. I paused from further injecting myself. I was trying to understand what was happening. I heard loud music, drums, tambourines, clapping, shouting. There were desperate cries for Jesus to help the children being repeated over and over again. There was also a great deal of other unintelligible preaching and praying coming through the wall beneath the stairs.

As the distressing sounds continued to fill the stairwell, I squeezed the syringe, sending the substance into my veins. I lost consciousness and slid down the wall until my head came to rest on the floor with my legs stretched out before me. Moments later, I regained a degree of consciousness and staggered from beneath the steps, and I left the building. I staggered over to the church. I sat beneath an archway in front of two large green double doors in front of the church. I sat there under the power of the drug, nodding, facing the street with my forearms on my knees, listening to the music that had now waned considerably. Then I heard a loud squeal; it sounded like wood splitting. It was the large green doors opening behind me. Fifty or sixty people began pouring out of the large doors, casually talking to each other. I was like a rock in a river. The crowd of people streamed around me. I was bumped and pushed by them walking past. Someone kicked me in the head, trying to step over me. It may have hurt, but I couldn't feel a thing. The people left the church and locked the doors behind them. They got into cars or hailed taxis; others faded into the night in small groups.

The prayers and cries to the Lord that I felt coming through the wall may have helped guide the course of my life in the right direction. I will never forget how their words and music seemed to come through the wall and inhabit my body, though only for a moment. They made a great impression upon me, but I had never been certain of what it all meant.

The Second Fisherman

Five years later a congregation in Harlem led by a street-wise pastor by the name of the Reverend Dr. William M. James, who practiced community outreach with intentionality, drew me into the back door of the church. He approached me in the Times Square area of New York City, well beyond the wall of safety between the church and the community. He did not introduce himself as a clergyman. Had he introduced himself as a pastor or reverend, I would have circled away from being caught and possibly escaped his plan. The average streetwise kid didn't have a good opinion about the church, and I was no exception. He engaged me in a conversation about some needs that I obviously had. He drew me in that way. He introduced me to people who were part of the ministries at his church. Rev. James also reached out to many other young people. He caught people from a variety of "waters" in life. Naturally, the circumstances presented to the members and leaders of the Metropolitan United Methodist Church challenged them. Everyone that was caught in the nets of the Back-Door Ministries didn't make it. I found the church to be patient, and I persevered. These programs assisted me to get back in school, find a job, and get a handle on all that I needed to do to move forward. The greatest aspect of this ministry was that it challenged me and many others to think about life from a spiritual and intellectual point of view. Over the course of time the encouragement of the congregation led me to walk through the front doors of the church, seeking salvation without shame or reservation.

The pastor's concealing his Christian label so as not to spook me was a clear sign of his wisdom. This encounter taught me that Christian language is not nearly as important as the spiritual awareness and concern to bring people to Christ. I didn't know this fisher of people's plan. I didn't have to know because I was the fish. The plan was revealed to me after I was well within the net.

Opening the Back Door Can Draw People through the Front Door

I met numerous community residents representing every profession. They became members of that church simply because they wanted an opportunity to be a part of or to support the congregation's community outreach. This experience made a lasting impression upon me, and as a result, I have always made community outreach an important part of how to grow my congregation. Inspiring the congregation to reach out to the community and providing training for people in the context of its needs invariably have led to church growth.

The back door of the church was important to outreach because few people coming through the traditional front door were oriented, trained, or equipped to deal with the sort of "fish" I had been, let alone reeling me into the church. Back-Door Ministries are one of a myriad of outreach ministries that will draw people through the front doors of the church.

From Back-Door Ministries to the Ordained Ministry

My life and ministry are the results of Back-Door Ministries, and I believe they continue to contribute to church growth. The church cannot afford *not* to have these ministries wherever they are needed.

My past experiences in the street, along with twenty-three years of serving the traditional churches, have enabled me to help them tighten the net of grace and love in the traditional church. I have helped many people who grew up in the traditional church to see that they have a lot more in common with people coming through the back doors than they have differences. Through interjecting my life story into preaching, I have reached the hearts and minds of longtime members of the church with the message that drugs and alcohol are not the problems. Sin is the problem, and until all are saved all are vulnerable to sin, however it manifests itself.

Church growth becomes possible when the church recognizes that the voice of Jesus Christ still has the power to call that which did not exist into existence (Romans 4:17). I know because it was the voice of Christ, working through the church, that called me forth from the grave.

I was called to ministry and became a staff member of Metropolitan UMC. Drew University, the Methodist City Society, and the New York Annual Conference recognized the significance of these ministries and supported them.

I had the opportunity of playing a key role in developing several community outreach programs that contributed to church growth. The programs were designed to reach young men and women in the community in both traditional and nontraditional ways (i.e., tutors, mentors, financial advisers, and family counselors). Services provided were temporary housing, psychological counseling, and life management seminars that inspired youth and young adults to go on to higher education. This ministry was responsible for helping 3,600 young people go to colleges and universities; 76 of them went into the ordained ministry. Many of the people who went to college through these ministries came back to the church after graduation and joined the church, bolstering its ministries and spurring church growth.

This program drew the interest of many other community residents and representatives of other organizations who wanted to make sure that our programs were supported. Congregations that develop outreach programs to address real problems, challenges, or needs of the community are perceived by the same community to be on target,

relevant, and desirable. Such congregations have the mag-
netism to draw people who may have given up on the
church.

People's hearts are touched, emotions are stirred, and
spirits are enlarged when they believe the church cares for
them. Every church should develop programs for the community. The number of fish that can be caught through
community outreach is limited only by the presence or
absence of nets. Churches that clean and tighten their nets
in the interest of effectively reaching people with God's
love will catch fish. Through community outreach, I have
seen and experienced how faith and hard work can bring
about the fulfillment of the scripture that says, "For those
who want to save their life will lose it, and those who lose
their life for my sake will find it" (Matthew 16:25).

PART FOUR

Spiritual Formation

CHAPTER EIGHT

LORD, LISTEN TO YOUR CHILDREN PRAYING

PLANNING, GUIDING, AND SUSTAINING SPIRITUAL FORMATION IN THE AFRICAN AMERICAN CONGREGATION FOR CHURCH GROWTH

Eugene A. Blair

Spiritual Formation: A Model for Church Growth

We live in a time of tremendous change and transformation in all sectors of our society. The strategic transformation of African American congregations to meet these changes is an ongoing process. It calls for major, profound, and irreversible changes in the congregation. This process must analyze, critique, and radically alter the fundamental ways of perceiving, believing, thinking, and behaving throughout all aspects of congregational life. It is a transformation of the congregation's spirit for ministry and growth. This process involves the entire church body and the way the members view themselves, their church, and the world. It is a shift from an established or declining church to a missionary community of African American believers.

This is church growth. I will describe for you a model to make this happen. Churches want to grow. Rarely do churches admit that they want to stagnate or decline. By carefully and intentionally selecting the right model for growth, any church can grow. Sometimes it is a matter of pointing out blocks and obstacles that can be removed in a matter of months. Sometimes congregations are in such a state of complacency or decline that more is needed. Often congregations want to reach new people for Christ but are not sure why or how.

Several congregational and biblical tasks are accomplished through a spiritual formation model. First, the church calls people to draw closer to God as the primary task for their lives. The people of God are on a spiritual journey to love and know God and one another in new and creative ways. By choosing a growth model based on spiritual formation, we signal to all the importance of putting God first in all that we do and say. Christian spiritual formation is everything we do after we say yes to Jesus.

Second, we unleash the spiritual power that is ours as the church and as individuals. By calling the church to an accountable life of prayer, nurturing, discipleship, and study, we connect ourselves to the giver of life and the source of the universe, God. The latest church growth gimmicks will not work. The hard work of growth and formation pays off in the gifts of the spirit that God offers to those who faithfully travel this road.

Finally, when we engage people in a ministry that changes their being, we see lives changed. When lives are changed, people have testimonies. They just have to tell somebody what God has done for them. Others want to know where they, too, can have their lives changed. When we come full circle and complete the task, the church grows in numbers and spirit.

When I was a child, it seemed that the Sunday service went on forever. It seemed to me that our pastor, the Reverend Council M. Harris, now deceased, preached sermons that lasted a lifetime. But every Sunday, without fail, his sermons ended the same way: "The doors of the church are now open." The invitation was to come and join the church, to become a Christian in response to the message just preached. We thought that he meant he was finally going to let us out of there!

At a young age, I responded to that message. Not only that, later in life I received a call to full-time Christian ministry. As an ordination gift, my local church gave me Rev. Harris's preaching robe, the robe he wore that day I became a member of the church. It reminds me of the day when he said, "The doors of the church are open," and I came down and took his hand. Many have taken the step to join the church and become a Christian. Arguably, they are two different things. Yet for most of us these were one and the same motion. But we are painfully aware that the masses in our day and time have a waning interest in the things of the institutional church or have left the church through the back door. Primary among the reasons is dissatisfaction with the lack of spiritual nurture and care of the soul.

The African American church has a unique and rich history in the American landscape. It is where the "souls of black folks" are nurtured and cared for. True, it is the place where we meet to praise and worship God, enjoy fellowship one with another, and prepare ourselves to move out into service to the world. Yet it is more. Spiritual formation is the "wheel in the middle of a wheel." It is at the center of the congregation, its heart and soul. It cannot be confined to a single program, group, or committee. The African American pastor knows that when the church *grows* spiritually, lives can be changed.

Too often, rather than drawing people closer to God, the busyness of church burns people out. As a result, they conclude that if this is spirituality, they do not need it. Think about it; people are very busy "serving the Lord," spending countless hours volunteering and giving. Yet many are spiritually starving on the inside. The church works hard to get people in the front door with promises of meaning and fulfillment, only to lose them through the back door by not caring for their souls.

What do people expect when they come to church? The answers are complex. But basically, people want to receive spiritual direction for their lives, and they come to church expecting help with this process. They want to discover their God-given gifts and spiritual graces. They want to feel and experience God in an alive and rewarding way. This experience can happen only when a congregation is about the business of developing an intentional ministry of congregational spiritual formation.

Beginning with conversion, spirituality is a process of cultivating a relationship with God that lasts a lifetime. It is an understanding that reaching spiritual maturity and nurturing one's journey is the primary task of one's life and the ministry of the church. The spiritual life of every member is a story that is revealed day by day.

Spiritual Formation in the African American Church

The primary task of the local African American church is to introduce people to Jesus Christ in creative and positive ways. The church must then disciple those who come into the faith so that they will know their role in bringing others to Christ. The African American church has the added central task of discipling black folks so they can understand their lives as Africans and Americans and what these realities mean in the context of their church, community, and world.

It is common practice throughout church history to describe the spiritual life within the context of a particular historical period or a single religious person or a theological tradition, as well as culturally, ethnically, or racially. These spiritualities often have a founder and teacher who called together followers. These followers or disciples followed certain teachings, and those teachings became institutionalized for later generations. The founder of Christian spirituality is Jesus of Nazareth.

Spirituality is "the style of a person's response to Christ before the challenge of everyday life, in a given historical and cultural environment." While the essence of spirituality is to encounter the Divine, there are particularities in that search. African American spirituality is one such particularity.[1]

Such a particularity as African American spiritual formation needs to be carefully defined. Spiritual (*to breathe*) formation (*to form, reflect the image of*) in the Christian context is the work of the Holy Spirit to transform our lives. The goal is to make us into saints, into the image of Jesus Christ. The New Testament spells out that image and how to obtain it, and what it means. Although there are many different spiritualities in the African American community, we are discussing Christian spirituality. Therefore, *African American spirituality is Africa based; it is the way we care for the souls of black folks in the sacred world we created through a collection of distinctive and vital characteristics, practices, disciplines, and values. All of this has been forged in the crucible of the lives of black folks with its attendant racism, oppression, and suffering. It is our response to the grace of God.*

In the context of the Christian community, African American spirituality is the way in which black folks understand the God of their lives and what it means to be followers of Jesus Christ. The common spirit and thread running through the various black and African American spiritualities are justice and righteousness, that God has the last word. It is an attitude of life and prayer that sees all of life as an encounter with a grace-filled, compassionate, and forgiving God.

In the local congregation, we have to recognize two fundamental ideas about spirituality. First, spiritual formation does not just happen. It is the work of the Holy Spirit. We must be intentional about inviting the Holy Spirit into planning processes, our boards, committees, and task forces. How often have we set about the work of the church with perfunctory prayer at the beginning and end of our regularly scheduled meetings? Just because we are a local Christian church does not mean that spiritual formation will happen automatically.

Second, every church, no matter what size, has to have an intentional and specific emphasis on spiritual formation. There must be a plan of some kind. Every church has the responsibility to take seriously the spiritual development and discipleship of each member. Empowered by prayer and surrounded by the Holy Spirit, every church can create and develop a plan to make this happen. All that the church does must be evaluated in terms of an established plan to disciple people in the faith and help them on their spiritual journeys.

The Role of the Pastor

The role of the pastor is key in this process of change and transformation. If you are the pastor, begin to pray about the spiritual journey of the congregation. Where is the Holy Spirit leading the congregation? This can be a challenge for those pastors who need to control and dominate the ministry of their local church. Spiritual formation is a permission-giving process, a process that allows the Holy Spirit to move in people's lives and make changes. As people grow and transform, so must the ministry of the church. Ask God to show you the needs and the opportunities to help this flock of God's people grow. Pray and ask yourself these important questions (you may want to keep a written journal of your responses and reflections):

- Who am I as the shepherd of this flock?
- Do the members view me as a person of prayer?
- Is my ministry informed first and foremost by the working of the Holy Sprit?
- Am I ready to allow a permission-giving process to take hold in the congregation?

The next step may be to call together a visioning or ministry team composed of persons who have a strong desire to be more intentional in their own spiritual growth. Emphasize the use of the term *ministry team* and not committee. This effort cannot be led by just another church committee. Nor is it just another layer of church structure. It must be led by persons who have a desire for and understand the need for spiritual renewal in their own lives and the life of the congregation.

At this point, you will want to have an informal conversation with them about their own journeys and visions for the congregation. Focus on these questions:

- What has been your individual spiritual journey?
- What have been important spiritual moments for you in this congregation?
- Who have been the most spiritually influential people in your life?

- What experiences have influenced you most on your spiritual journey?
- What is different for you about the African American church?
- How can this church meet the spiritual needs of its members?

Subsequent meetings may then be called to consider some visions shared by the group. At that time, you will want to share some ideas put forth in this book and other resources. Share your hopes for the spiritual vitality of the congregation. Be specific and keep notes on all the sharing. There are no "bad ideas" at this point. Keep the meeting open and encourage everyone to share. You want to know how, as an African American church, this congregation can foster spiritual growth.

Get down to making some decisions for the future. Ask the group for guidance in these next steps. You may want to expand the group. Here are some options for next steps:

- Request the official board or council to prayerfully support and encourage a new ministry team on spiritual formation.
- Make this book and other resources available to the appropriate people.
- Organize the meeting schedule for the team.
- Prayerfully seek a layperson to lead the team.
- Collect resources and materials for the team.
- Organize a churchwide prayer effort about this ministry.

Role of the Layperson

While the role of the pastor cannot be overemphasized, lay leadership is essential in this process of planning. Empowering laypeople to pray and grow in their spiritual life is what this is all about. Many efforts of the local church fail because inadequate attention has been given to the training and incorporating of laity. Make an appointment to share your interest in spiritual formation with your pastor. If the pastor is not familiar with this book, give him or her a copy, and request that the two of you share your thoughts about this and other books. Take the initiative and volunteer to help plan the meetings for the visioning group.

When the spiritual formation team is appointed, take an active part. The name of the team will communicate to the congregation at large that a new thrust is about to take place. Be ready at all times to interpret this movement. Members of this new team must be ready to become advocates for spiritual formation within the life of the congregation. They will want to work with other standing committees in the planning and promoting of this new thrust. Communication is the key to success and support. Keep everyone informed about what is in store for the congregation. *Your basic task is to be a dynamic spiritual presence and force in the life of the congregation sounding the call to be more intentional about the spiritual journey.*

The spiritual life team will not necessarily be adding new programs to the life of the church. The team will be responsible for adding a new emphasis to the program life of the church and for coordinating all events and emphases through the proper channels. Do not overlook the evaluating stage of any new thrust in the church. The spiritual life team is responsible to the governing body of the church for reporting all programs, plans, and evaluations. This should include recommendations about what the congregation may want to change, adjust, or eliminate from the present ministry in order to make spiritual formation a priority within the life of the church.

Most new programs and new forms of ministry begin as experimental ministries and pilot projects. Allow time for the congregation to adjust and respond to these new ideas. There must be flexibility and openness. Above all, and through all, saturate all spiritual formation efforts with prayer. Constantly seek divine guidance.

A Three-Year Plan for Spiritual Formation

No matter where it is located or how large, God has a plan for every local church. God wants every local church to be in effective ministry in its little corner of the world. Each church is unique and must create its own approach for deepening the spirituality of its people. It cannot be said too often that every church must pray and seek the leadership and guidance of the Holy Spirit to discern what God's plan is for it. No church can shrug off the necessity of creative planning for an intentional emphasis on spiritual formation.

A three-year plan is recommended in order to move a church forward and to achieve long-lasting results. Some churches will need to move from no planning for spiritual formation while others may need to move beyond planning for program activities. In spiritual formation, events have their place. The difference between events and activities has to do with the intention of the program. Events are designed with an anticipated outcome beyond "busyness." Spiritual formation events are *formative* when they are planned to facilitate an overall vision of growth and development. The spiritual formation emphasis in your church will be enhanced as your team begins to look beyond present activities and programs.

To get started, let your team spend some time answering three key questions:

1. How would you describe the spiritual climate of our church right now?
2. What kind of church do we want to be three years from now?
3. What are you willing to do and how are you willing to change to make this happen?

The question for the team is not, What do we want to be doing [activities]? but What do we want to be three years from now? The latter is a formative question. These questions should be properly considered in the context of the African American church and the essential qualities of personal and corporate servanthood and discipleship. When your team can clearly articulate the vision, share it with the governing body. Take as long as necessary to guide the leaders of your church in further shaping this vision so that it can be commonly owned by everyone.

Every church has its own points of entry and learning. I want to identify six key starting points readily available to any local church. These starting points are already built into the program fabric of most churches. With some intentional planning, these can become the basis for a deeper spiritual journey for the congregation. Take into account the following and build on:

- Preaching and worship through the liturgical year
- Bible study and the Common Lectionary
- Intentional prayer ministry
- African and African American cultural and religious events
- Small groups
- Intentional mission and outreach

The Liturgical Year

The liturgical year is sometimes referred to as the Christian year. Denominations and judicatories have produced several resources to assist us in understanding the liturgical year. Keeping time by Sundays is an ancient church process of spiritual formation. This, too, is the tradition of the black church. For example, we use Sundays and not dates to keep time: "Our church anniversary is the fourth Sunday in June," or "Our choir day is the second Sunday in May."

Even the most casual church attendees will notice that the vestments on the altar and pulpit change with the Christian seasons. Perhaps they will notice that the pastor's or the choir's stole is a signal that a change has taken place. Your team can seize this opportunity to teach and guide the congregation in a new way by using these seasonal themes. Altar paraments, clergy stoles, choir robes, church school lessons, and liturgical themes and colors are guides to the meaning of the seasons of the Christian year. These can also be guides to new and different opportunities for spiritual development and growth.

You may want to consider special emphases and events in such a way that you can take advantage of the liturgical season. For example:

- Advent—call attention to personal devotional time in the home.
- Christmas—emphasize global spirituality and global peace.
- Epiphany—underscore the role of the family in spiritual formation.
- Lent—focus on prayer and worship attendance with a prayer vigil.
- Easter—emphasize corporate disciplines of worship and confession.
- Pentecost—study the Holy Spirit and the use of spiritual gifts in ministry of the church.

This is a time to be creative and open to new ideas. You may want to use the church school or weeknight study groups as a base for these events. Involve as many groups and people as possible in leadership roles.

The Common Lectionary

Many denominations and the Roman Catholic Church use what is referred to as the Common Lectionary for worship, study, and devotions. The Lectionary for Sundays and festivals is arranged as a guide for celebrating the Christian year and the reading and study of scripture in a systematic and coherent fashion in a three-year cycle:

- Year A is often referred to as the year of Matthew.
- Year B, the year of Mark.
- Year C, the year of Luke.

The Lectionary will guide readers through the Bible in a way that will help us "keep time" with the life of Jesus Christ. The Lectionary for each Sunday of the year provides an Old Testament reading, a psalm, a selection from the Epistles, and a gospel reading.

The Lectionary helps structure Christian worship on a recurring rhythm of the church's year. It can be broadened to encompass study, prayer, and meditation. We do not have to be locked into the Lectionary. There is a great deal of flexibility in terms of how we use these readings for each Sunday. Here are some ideas about how to use scripture in a programmatic way:

1. Lead a series of studies on the prayer life of Jesus.
2. Lead a series of studies on the disciples and their lives.
3. Conduct a preaching series on the parables or the Beatitudes.
4. Lead a seasonal Bible study on the selected texts for that season. For example, lead a Bible study each week of Advent on the gospel texts for the coming Sunday.
5. Conduct an overnight retreat to begin each season. Share the scripture texts for that season, and have a time of prayer for the congregation and personal and corporate growth.

One task of your team is to study the liturgical year and inform your congregation about the value of the Common

Lectionary. There should never be "just another Sunday." Every worship service should be offered to the congregation after a season of prayer, preparation, and highest level of participation. Worshipers ought to be able to leave the worship event and speak to others about the theme, content, and spirit that took place in the service or events.

Intentional Prayer Ministries

Our spirituality is a spirituality of prayer. As we pray for ourselves, one another, and the human condition, we find a corporate and personal balance in our lives and ministries. This balance is maintained through acts of intercession and encouragement, worship and praise, fellowship and community, and a healthy maintenance of the mind, body, and spirit.

Finding this balance is the call to nurture and care for the souls of black folks. This, in a word, is African American spirituality. It is not African spirituality nor is it American spirituality. It is a third entity rooted in Africa and the African American church, and it is informed by the nature and practice of black theology. These form the sacred world of black folks and the black church where its values, disciplines, gifts, and ministry are kept and nurtured as means of grace. All of this is the culture of prayer in the tradition of the black church.

Who can forget the images of Martin Luther King, Jr., and his followers praying in churches before going out to face the real life of racism in Alabama and other places? The movement of liberation in America was born in the prayers of the church as uttered from the mouths of God's people.

We, too, must call ourselves into "an attitude of prayer." We can and must do this through the following:

- Prayer circles and prayer bands
- Calls to pray for the events and life of the congregation
- Calls to persons to pray daily for themselves, the church, and the world
- Ongoing prayer teams for the program, pastor, and worship life of the church
- Prayer for persons who are sick, hospitalized, or unable to leave their homes
- Instruction for individuals about how to simply pray for themselves and their lives

We must give people permission to pray! Sounds strange? Maybe, but the pastor is not the only person who can pray when persons are sick, during worship, before meals, or in an emergency. We need not run and get the pastor when a need for prayer arises. Teaching people to pray must be an essential part of the formative life of the congregation. It is time to get back to the basics.

African American Events and Special Days

There is no better way to care for the souls of black folks than to celebrate the events that have shaped and secured their place in history. The African American church can reclaim its role as the resting place for black folks on this journey by reclaiming that which is already ours. Holidays have replaced holy days, those times when we historically emphasized worship, the liturgy, and care for the spirit. Now, too often holidays are just days off from work.

By giving new meaning to these special days, individuals and the church can be nurtured in the faith. A dynamic process of formation can be extracted from these days and events with careful and intentional planning. Place prayer, worship, and fellowship at the center. Use these special times for added services and celebrations, retreats, days of prayer and silence, acts of reflection, and acts of service. Such days might include:

- Martin Luther King, Jr., Day (a national holiday)
- Black History Month
- Women in History Month
- International Women's Day
- Rites of passage for boys and girls
- Juneteenth celebrations
- African festivals and cultural events
- Black arts and film festivals
- Independence days of African nations and Kwanza
- Mother's Day, Father's Day, Grandparents Day (a celebration of the elders)
- New Year's Day (a significant celebration in most African nations)
- A churchwide pilgrimage to Africa

These are the kinds of events and special days that can have a lasting effect on the spiritual growth of individuals and the African American church. Our people yearn for a connection to Africa and their American history. Using special days and celebrations can make that connection.

Small Groups: A Vital Link

The ministry of small groups is a vital channel for spiritual formation. The value of small groups in the local church for personal and corporate formation cannot be overstated. The Christian faith cannot be fully experienced in isolation. Ours is a communal spirituality. No matter what your plan, you must plan to include small groups.

Small groups provide key settings for dynamic movement in the spiritual life of persons who welcome opportunities to grow. Various needs can be met for a variety of persons when the local church provides a small groups ministry. When there is a felt need, there is an opportunity to form a group to meet that need.

When thinking about small groups, the best strategy question is *not,* How can we start more small groups in the church? The question should be, What identifiable needs do people have in common, and is this congregation called to meet those needs? It is important to read the literature and resources available on the church's ministry with small groups. In order for small groups to be successful, leaders need to be trained. Not everyone can lead others in a ministry such as this.

The dynamics of the small-group process, while identifiable, can be complex. Frustration, failure, and disappointment can be the fruit of our labor unless we understand the stages of the life of a group and when a group is working or is dysfunctional. There are identifiable reasons why some groups are healthy and some are not. Groups may go through several stages of gathering, pain, and growth.

Some of the stages are essential while others are not. Prayerfully enter this ministry so that you do no harm by being poorly prepared for the tasks of small groups and the people's lives that will be affected.

Some Ideas for Small Groups and Spiritual Growth Groups

- New membership groups that turn into church school classes
- Prayer and Bible study–centered groups
- Groups centered on a book or specific study
- Groups using workbooks and small group studies
- Spiritual formation in the family—events and groups for the whole family
- Sharing and fellowship groups
- Age-sensitive groups, such as youth, men, or women with young children
- Themes such as Africa, art, or spiritual dance
- Twelve step groups, health concerns, older adults

No group should be proposed without a defined time frame, clear expectations, publicity, and recruitment. It is important for the group to honor the time frame once it has been established. All groups need enthusiastic and trained leaders. Again, intentional reading of the literature on group process and ministry is very important. Working with groups in the church should not be taken lightly.

In our culture, "groups" are the norm of the day. From twelve step support groups to women's Bible studies, small groups have become a mainstay of spiritual formation ministry in the church. In order to disciple persons in the faith, there must be support, accountability, and commitment through small groups that will encourage minimum disciplines in the corporate and personal life journey.

Intentional Mission and Outreach

We have all heard it said numerous times, "We had church today!" Our next question is often, "Well, what did the preacher say?" The response too often is, "I don't know, but we sure had church!" This kind of conversation takes place every Sunday after church. It reminds us all that *everything* we do must be directed toward making disciples for Jesus Christ. We cannot just talk about "having church." We must do and be the church. One way of approaching this idea of intentional mission and ministry is to ask the question, What good are we trying to do for whom?

In other words, we must ask, Who are the people we are trying to reach, and why do we want to reach them? We cannot call people to a spiritual journey unless we know who they are and why we want to issue that call. The church's vision, mission, and mission plan are the place to start and the road map to our destination. Our intentional plan must include the following:

- Worship—make it emotive, relevant, vital, and dynamic.
- Spiritual gifts assessments—help persons discover their God-given gifts.

- Intentional discipleship—establish a directed education program to make disciples for Christ of new believers, helping them use their God-given gifts.
- Leadership—develop strategic lay leadership to meet the vision, helping people employ their God-given gifts.
- Vital relationships—help people love their family, friends, and God.
- Integrated stewardship—ensure that there is a holistic and ongoing ministry of lay involvement, using time, talents, and gifts throughout the year.
- Families—strengthen and equip them to care for themselves.
- Intentional and directed community outreach—support strategic and intentional outreach to unchurched people.
- Basic and advanced Bible study—provide opportunities for study.

If God blessed your congregation with all of the new members you desire, you have to answer the question, What do we want to happen to them because they are in our church? Further, what is our plan to make this happen, and how will we know we have succeeded? All of this calls for an intentional plan of mission and ministry.

Choosing Your Emphases

You are now ready to get specific and select the emphases that will implement your vision. How many spiritual emphases are reasonable for the size of your membership? Here is a guide to help you.

A Small Membership Church

You may choose one spiritual formation emphasis a year. For example, a new congregation may choose a theme of new life or a "building the body of Christ" theme. A congregation that is redeveloping may choose a theme of rebirth in Jesus Christ. An older congregation experiencing new life may consider new wine in new wineskins.

A Medium-sized Membership Church

You may choose one emphasis every three to six months. For example, you may choose a New Testament theme for study and preaching over the summer months. Then choose a new theme and emphasis for the fall months, and so on throughout the year.

A Large Membership Church

You may want to select a major emphasis every two to three months. There may be several events and opportunities for growth going on at the same time. At various times during the year, offer several special electives or options.

Your congregational vision will inform your decisions. Your emphases will determine your program and events in spiritual formation. At this point in your planning, your team can make responsible and far-reaching decisions about the church calendar and budget for spiritual formation in your church.

The old adage is true in this process: *if you fail to plan, you plan to fail.* Plan on providing a life-changing ministry to your spiritually hungry congregation. Every step of the way must be submitted to a rigorous evaluation. Get honest feedback from the participants and members. Never forget that God has a plan for your church. Pray that God would continue to reveal that plan to you. That plan calls for spiritual growth, change, and outreach to the unchurched.

God listens when we pray. We have not, because we do not ask. Ask God to give you and your church a vision of change and growth. Open the scriptures and study the word. Open your hearts and receive the Spirit. You will not be disappointed.

Note

1. Katherine Marie Dyckman and L. Patrick Carroll, *Inviting the Mystic, Supporting the Prophet: An Introduction to Spiritual Direction* (New York: Paulist Press, 1981), 73.

CHAPTER NINE

THE DEPTH OF OUR LOVE FOR CHRIST DETERMINES THE LEVEL OF OUR COMMITMENT TO SPIRITUAL FORMATION

D. Lovett Sconiers

So I say, live by the Spirit, and you will not grat-
ify the desires of the sinful nature. For the sinful
nature desires what is contrary to the Spirit, and
the Spirit what is contrary to the sinful nature.
... But the fruit of the Spirit is love, joy, peace,
patience, kindness, goodness, faithfulness, gen-
tleness and self-control. (Galatians 5:16-17, 22-23
NIV)

During my twenty years of walking with the Lord as
a born-again believer and serving in ministry
throughout the country, the Lord has imparted to
me the grave importance of "living by and walking in

135

love," the firstfruit of the Spirit. Being born again for me means that I have developed what the Reverend Dr. Carlyle Fielding Stewart III terms a "kingdom consciousness," indicating that I have become aware of God's presence in all of my endeavors, and the shaping of my beliefs and actions is based on this awareness.[1]

Being rooted in love and concern for humanity as a genuine creature of God empowers me to help mend the brokenness and alienation emanating from human sin in the world through my preaching, teaching, and counseling ministries. The dynamic principle operating at the core of God's purpose being harmonized for all creation is love: love of self, love of God, and love of others. Love and concern constitute the principal substance out of which relations in the church are built.[2] Love as a foundation is one of the primary principles of spiritual formation in the church, which governs our passions and our compassions. Dr. Stewart declares that these two traits are the first marks of prophetic church growth because passionate and compassionate people actively seek the recovery of lost souls.[3] These traits are a necessity in making the church healthy and vital, in addition to enhancing church growth.

It was in the hallowed halls of Harvard Divinity School that God brought Dr. Stewart into my life as a spiritual big brother while he was on sabbatical there as a Merrill Fellow working on one of his many books. Dr. Stewart also came to recognize me as a "sojourner who was not ashamed to be used by the Holy Ghost!" I felt honored when he made this dedication to me in his dynamic book *Reclaiming What Was Lost: Recovering Spiritual Vitality in the Mainline Church.*[4] His book gave a voice to my sentiments and struggles on my tedious journey as a woman of God committed to walking in the beauty of holiness, according to Paul's exhortation in Romans 12: "Therefore, I urge you, brothers [sisters], in view of God's mercy, to offer your bodies as living sacrifices, holy and pleasing to God—this is your spiritual act of worship.... Love must be sincere. Hate what is evil; cling to what is good" (vv. 1, 9 NIV).

Jesus' emphasis on cultivating our inner strength signifies the importance of inner spiritual development for the achievement of our authentic existence. Through the practice of spiritual discipline, we as believers realize that the liberating power of God resides at the core of our inner being.[5] When we are born again, we begin to comprehend God's great purpose for the human race. One of the first things that God does is to propel his concern for the whole world through the channels of our hearts. Thus, the love of God, even his very nature, is manifested in us. The objective side of spiritual regeneration is the sacrificial act of Christ's display of his passionate love in coming to die for the sins of the world. This is evidenced in the most comprehensive statement of the gospel of Jesus Christ as found in the New Testament scripture John 3:16. The origin of this verse is the love of God for the world; its manifestation is the gift of his only begotten Son; and its purpose, which reveals the nature of Almighty God, is focused on the salvation of all who choose to believe in Christ—"For God so loved the world...."

The gospel writer John clarifies the importance of *passion and compassion* in our identifying with Christ when he states

Jesus' "divine commandment": "I am giving you a new command. You must love each other, just as I have loved you. If you love each other, everyone will know that you are my disciples" (John 13:34-35 CEV). Christian discipleship is best observed when church communities visibly identify themselves with God's interest in other people. In his book *How Black Is the Gospel?* Tom Skinner wrote, "In terms of the spiritual wealth that it takes to make a man a man, what makes a man a real man is his ability to love."[6]

The ongoing challenge for me as an African American pastor serving in an African Methodist Episcopal (AME) church, while also serving as a college chaplain and religion professor in an AME-founded and -funded college, is to "walk in love." In an effort to effectively fulfill my responsibility for the faith formation and spiritual growth and development of the students, the faculty and staff, and my parishioners, the summary of the Ten Commandments is an ever-present principle governing my daily life:

> Jesus replied: " 'Love the Lord your God with all your heart and with all your soul and with all your mind.' This is the first and greatest commandment. And the second is like it: 'Love your neighbor as yourself.' All the Law and the Prophets hang on these two commandments." (Matthew 22:37-40 NIV)

Serving in all of these arenas, I find that it is impossible to fake love. It is not enough for me just to preach and teach love; I am compelled to practice it as well. Young people have a way of knowing when you are, as they say, "keeping it real!"

According to Dr. Stewart, a key to prophetic ministry is the cultivation of a vocabulary of caring, a vocabulary that is vitally connected to the critical issues of those to whom such love is given.[7] In order for us to care, we must have compassion and passion for those to whom we are sent to serve. This passion is expressed as our genuine concern for the well-being and wholeness of others. Thus, I am compelled daily to live by the Reverend Dr. Martin Luther King, Jr.'s thematic topic "love in action." In King's book *Strength to Love*, he described the task of believers needing to bring together our head and our heart, intelligence and goodness, in order to rise to the fulfillment of our true nature. To rise to this fulfillment, King emphasized the integration of the spiritual and the intellectual. In the foreword to her husband's book *Strength to Love*, Coretta Scott King said that "love, truth, and the courage to do what is right should be our own guideposts on this lifelong journey."[8]

While I was attending Harvard from 1988 to 1991, the Lord revealed to me how the combination of "spirituality and intellectuality" can be manifested in our lives as spiritual leaders. Prior to my answering my call to ministry, I was practicing law in Washington, D.C., which I gave up out of my love for God to do full-time ministry. My prophetic conviction resulted in an irrepressible desire for me to "live God's Word." This was the persuasion that empowered me to take such a drastic action. Unlike the rich lawyer who dialogued with Jesus about eternal life in the nineteenth chapter of Matthew, I gave up everything to follow Christ. My family thought I had lost my mind, and if they had had power of attorney, they probably would have had me committed. However, in the words of Max Lucado, my love of Christ leaves me no choice.[9]

Before I entered Harvard, the Lord made sure that I was Spirit-filled as well as rooted and grounded in his word because he knew that I was going to be fire-baptized through various trials at the university. My presence on the campus was a beacon light that caused a bit of confusion among most of the white students and my professors, most of whom were published theologians. They appeared to have limited knowledge that the Holy Spirit still empowers us; thus, they acted as if they had never witnessed the manifestation of the combination of "spirituality and intellectuality." Their ongoing question was, "How can you be an intelligent lawyer and be so full of the Holy Spirit?" I recall a very painful experience in one of my preaching classes with a white professor, who accused me of having too much passion when I delivered a sermon in class. He actually reduced my grade on the sermon from an A to a B.

I concur wholeheartedly with Dr. Stewart's assertion that in white denominations in general, black clergy observe an apparent devaluation, contempt, or suspicion of any ethos that resembles the rhythms, forms, and expressions of black life and culture. The Reverend Dr. Henry Mitchell contends that responsible, enthusiastic celebration during our preaching is far from anti-intellectual.[10] However, in this particular professor's class, my show of enthusiasm and emotion in the pulpit was synonymous with my losing control. On the contrary, in black culture, such an expression means "letting the Spirit flow."[11]

By the time I graduated from Harvard in 1991, most of my professors and the students had come to respect the presence and the power of God in my life, even though they still did not really understand me. Their response to me also affirms Dr. Stewart's contention that the corroborative function of African American spirituality is the reaffirmation of black intelligence amid conditions of racial mythologization. It is also congruous with the actualization of the black mind in positive response to white America in the face of psychological and cultural untruths.[12]

An objective of African American spirituality has been to instill in black people a self-love and self-respect that is rooted in God's divine love.[13] In addition to being baffled by the combination of my "spirituality and intellectuality," the faculty, staff, and student body at Harvard also raised their eyebrows at my self-love. Having the audacity to wear a very, very short Afro haircut for the past twenty years, amid conditions of hostility, persecution, discrimination, repression, rejection, and devaluation, exhibited that I had learned to love myself unconditionally as an African American female, maintain my dignity, and center myself spiritually. It was evident to everyone who met me at Harvard that I was (and am) very comfortable and content being a black woman. Centering ourselves in the all-enveloping love of God is a principal task of black spirituality. For me to love myself, when virtually everything in society has taught me to hate myself, demonstrated my quintessential attainment of African American freedom, according to Dr. Stewart's assertion: "Despite the negativity propagated by the media about the problems, troubles, and disparities of African Americans, the truth is there is a unifying, unquenchable love and kinship among those who are comfortable being black."[14]

At Harvard, I also had the privilege of taking courses from the late Reverend Dr. Samuel DeWitt Proctor, who was a well-published theologian, an anointed preacher, a college professor, and an international lecturer. Dr. Proctor became my spiritual mentor and the adviser for my senior thesis. One of our required reading assignments in his class was his *Preaching about Crises in the Community*. In his book, Proctor contends,

> If our commitment to Christ is formal, and perfunctory, our personal inadequacies as African American ministers will remain glaring. However, when we work towards getting closer to the Lord in our *love* for Him, we can increase our capacity to respond to the concerns of our congregations when parishioners seek refuge for their hurting souls.[15]

The good news of the gospel should challenge believers to lead a life that is obedient to God's word and that appropriates the power of God's love in us toward helping others. The jazz artist John Coltrane would call this *A Love Supreme*.[16] The Holy Spirit working in us does for us what no legalism from without could ever do. The Holy Spirit equips us with a new personhood, a new self, a distinct moral content centered in love that is not sentimental, but it is a commitment to action on our part. This new understanding through our Christian experience provides us with an ultimate moral control from within. It also provides us with a new life that manifests itself in love and service, which emphasizes both evangelism and social action.

Today, a changed society is calling for changed persons who are willing to work toward social actions as well as evangelism in order to relieve some of life's suffering and to correct most injustices. Spiritual leaders need a desire to honor God with a life of commitment and sacrifice, in order to permit God's redeeming love to be manifested in our public affairs. We have observed strong Spirit-filled Christians in the forefront of the antislavery movement, the women's suffrage movement, and the civil rights movement. These Christians were Spirit-led, and their values were shaped and formed by the Holy Spirit. The church needs this same level of spirituality today. Dr. Stewart wrote, "If the mainline church is going to reclaim and strengthen God's church, then it must adopt a plan for spiritual wellness and vitality as important hallmarks of healthy congregations and healthy leaders."[17]

If we believe what Matthew 7:16 teaches us—"By their fruit you will recognize them" (NIV)—then having spiritual wellness is synonymous to both pastors and laity being healthy fruit bearers in order for the church to grow. The Council of Bishops of the AME Church recently undertook the task of clarifying the direction in which they hope to lead our denomination. This task concluded with their adopting a quadrennial theme of *Living Well*, emphasizing wellness in four areas: spiritual, physical, intellectual, and emotional. They published the theme in *The Anvil: The Annual Resource Guide for Our Quadrennial*. This type of wholeness should be the impetus for spiritual vitality that will enable black churches to survive and succeed in the future.

In the spiritual foundation of our self-esteem, asserts Dr. Robert Wicks, one of my doctoral professors at Loyola College, one fruit is the freedom to be in relationship with others in a healthy, loving, and helpful way.[18] In order for pastors and laity to build and lead growing, healthy African American congregations, their spiritual formation requires three aspects of the spiritual gift of love in their lives: motivation *by* love, manifestation *of* love, and transformation *by* love.

A Motivation by Love Is Necessary for Spiritual Formation in Churches

> A new command I give you: Love one another. As I have loved you, so you must love one another. By this [everyone] will know that you are my disciples, if you love one another. (John 13:34-35 NIV)

An important gift that was exemplified by the biblical prophets and has proved helpful to those who have built vital and prophetic ministries is personal investment that is motivated by passion and conviction. Not only are passion and conviction considered to be hallmarks of prophetic ministries but also a desire to fully and unequivocally invest oneself in serving the Lord is absolutely necessary.

The passionate love of Christ is an incarnation of God's investment of himself, which led to Jesus' suffering and sacrifice on Calvary's cross for our sins. In an act of love Jesus emptied himself of some of his divinity to take on our humanity, as he came into the world as a newborn baby. Through prayer, meditation on God's word, and fasting, we must empty ourselves of our humanity in order to take on more of God's divinity. A famous axiom by Dietrich Bonhoeffer states, "When Christ calls a man, He bids him come and die."[19] This means that our love for God should motivate us to die to everything within us that does not honor and glorify God. This requires us, as Paul says in Hebrews 12:1 (NIV), to "throw off everything that hinders and the sin that so easily entangles" us, those ungodly things, habits, and people in our lives that separate our souls from our Savior as well as hinder our spiritual growth. Our love for God must permeate all of our motives such that all that we do honors and glorifies him. This is possible only when the Holy Spirit manifests his personality in us because the "fruit of the Spirit" is the work of the Holy Spirit in us, through us, and often in spite of us.

A "walk in love" is a by-product of being Christ-centered and Spirit-controlled once we have yielded our lives to God by accepting Christ as our Savior and Lord of our lives. In Matthew 22:37, Jesus declared to the rich young lawyer without hesitation that love is the supreme and divine requirement. The love that Jesus describes recognizes and makes a commitment to adhere to that which is righteous, true, and praiseworthy, regardless of our feelings about the matter.

When people are not motivated by love, they have a natural tendency to see only the faults and failures in others instead of looking for good in their personalities. There is a tendency to focus more on the shortcomings or weaknesses of others instead of their strengths. When the majority of a church congregation is not "walking in love," it is extremely difficult, if not impossible, to maintain unity within the body without a significant amount of strife and backbiting. Love and reverence for truth are two principles that constitute the foundation of all ethical actions. Once believers internalize them, love and truth affirm, motivate, and impel us toward our final consummation in community. The practice of love in relation with others should facilitate a movement toward spiritual unity within the church.

Relationships promote a kinship or bond between African Americans, where our humanity connects soul to soul, and where belonging emerges among us. This type of kinship is created only by the power of the divine Spirit, whose love and truth permeate the universe: "And above all these [put on] love and enfold yourselves with the bond of perfectness [which binds everything together completely in ideal harmony]" (Colossians 3:14 AMP).

Loving others as much as Christ loves others is a revolutionary act because it requires our love to be based on the sacrificial love that Jesus has shown us. This kind of love helps to keep Christians strong in a hostile world and to draw unbelievers into the body of Christ. With this kind of love, there is a radical shift in the focus of our wills, which helps us to yield all our desires to one overriding passion of letting God's "will be done" in our lives so that his Kingdom can come on earth (Matthew 6:10).

While serving as an associate pastor of a small, but rapidly growing AME church in Columbia, Maryland, in 1997,

I made this type of radical shift in my will out of my love for God and young people. The spirit of the Lord moved on my heart to organize a Girl Power Mentoring Program for at-risk young ladies who were from dysfunctional homes and on the verge of being suspended or expelled from school. I was motivated by the death of a high school teacher who had a heart attack while attempting to break up an altercation between two African American female students. When the news media reported the incident, I asked the question out of embarrassment and frustration, "Where were the mentors?" The response at the time was that there were none actively involved in the schools. I kept thinking that *someone* needed to organize a mentoring program to alleviate those types of incidents. The Lord kept it heavily on my heart for weeks until I could not keep silent any longer.

Of course, the *someone* became me, and I spoke up with the vision that the Lord had revealed to me. By working in conjunction with a local high school and female volunteers from the church, I became the founder and coordinator of the program in 1997. It had a major impact within the church as well as in the lives of the young ladies and their families who participated in the program. It was very painful and stressful at times working with the students who had severe behavioral problems. I made a lot of sacrifices as I diligently recruited and trained mentors, coordinated tutorial classes, and made arrangements for cultural, social, and educational activities for the young ladies. Every time I tried to terminate the program, God continued to pour out his love into my heart, which compelled me to persevere in faith.

Even though the Lord moved me from Maryland back to my home state of Florida in 1999, the program is still going strong several years after its inception. I received a recent praise report that ten of the young ladies with whom I began working are now in college. There is no way that I could have known that my obedience and loving concern would have motivated ten at-risk young women to stay in school, stay out of jail or a detention center, and ultimately go to college. The world's most powerful motivation is the sense of being loved. "When nothing else could help / Love lifted me."[20]

A Manifestation of Love Is Necessary for Spiritual Formation in Churches

> Now I will show you the most excellent way.... But [if I] have not love, I am nothing.... Now these three remain: faith, hope and love. But the greatest of these is love. (1 Corinthians 12:31–13:2, 13 NIV)

The love addressed in the New Testament is the love that takes the initiative in striving to create good in the lives of others. It is an active love, not passive or static. Apostle Paul dedicated the entire thirteenth chapter of his first letter to the church at Corinth on the topic of their conducting themselves in love. Spiritual gifts are not for individual self-advancement but for the church. God endows us with them for serving him, strengthening and enhancing the spiritual growth of the body of Christ.

However, most Christians appear to have a tendency to covet spiritual gifts that are showy. In order to be beneficial to the body of Christ, Paul recommends that we set our hearts on gifts that are not showy. He further describes love as "the most excellent way." The other spiritual gifts are described as being transitory, but only love endures.

As he pens the thirteenth chapter, Paul interpolates into his discussion of spiritual gifts a superb digression on the topic of love. Paul defines "real love" as the thing that gives reality and meaning to all the other spiritual gifts. Unless the other spiritual gifts are saturated in love as a supreme excellence, which is really the sublimation of the principle of forbearance, those who possess these gifts are nothing. Great faith exemplified by acts of dedication and miracle-working power produces very little within the body of Christ without love.

Christianity is the only religion in the world based on love in addition to faith and hope. Faith, hope, and love, Paul writes, are the only graces that last. Of the three, love is the only grace that is superior because it is divine. Faith without love is cold. Love is the fire that kindles our faith. Faith and hope are derived from our human nature; they depend on something outside us and expect some good to come to us. On the contrary, love is derived from God; it does not originate on its own accord. The love of God in us owes its existence to our contact with the Holy Spirit. In Romans 5:5, Paul writes, "God has poured out his love into our hearts by the Holy Spirit" (NIV).

In many of my theological discussions with Dr. Stewart in 1990, he often teased me about being so compassionate about my ministry. Even when I was a young child and people would hurt my feelings, my mother would caution me, saying, "Baby, you just love too hard." Of course, I did not have a clue about what she meant until after I was born again and came to understand how God manifests the spiritual fruit of love in our lives.

The Reverend Dr. Robert Franklin, another one of my Harvard professors, elaborated on the Reverend Dr. Martin Luther King, Jr.'s analogy of the geometric cube. Dr. Franklin discussed King's understanding of *personal integration,* which is a necessary component of spiritual formation in building a vital African American congregation. Dr. Franklin asserted that the theological virtues of faith, hope, and love were present in King's thoughts and life.

> Possession of the capacity to bear difficulties with patience, to face unjust treatment with a sense of certitude that injustice cannot reign forever, and to forgive the oppressor while never dehumanizing him or her, through this necessary virtue, we can discover the degree of a person's love for self, our neighbors, and God.[21]

These traits help believers to experience reconciliation, which is profoundly redemptive because it signifies God's healing of the fragmentation and conflict that divide the self, as well as the conflict and alienation that separate human beings from each other and hinder our love for one another. Reconciliation is a means of intimating care and concern for others in order to exemplify the degree to which God's redemptive love is actualized in our human relations.

A Transformation by Love Is Necessary for Spiritual Formation in Churches

> Dear friends, let us love one another, for love comes from God. Everyone who loves has been born of God and knows God. Whoever does not love does not know God, because God is love. (1 John 4:7-8 NIV)

Love is the most powerful and painful human emotion that we possess. People have gone to great lengths trying to express their love through poetry and music. However, our morally corrupt society often confuses love and lust. Unlike lust, Christlike love is directed outward toward helping others, not inward toward our selfish desires. This kind of love is contrary to our natural inclinations. We are able to set aside our own desires so that we can give love unselfishly without expecting anything in return. Our passion and compassion can bypass the world's deception in order to create a context for the transformative discovery of God's Word within church communities.[22]

While I served as the assistant to the pastor at Bethel AME Church in Massachusetts, God permitted me to observe his transforming power of love through the Reverend Dr. Ray Hammond and his wife and copastor, the Reverend Dr. Gloria White-Hammond, both medical doctors. Out of Pastor Ray's love for God, he gave up his medical career as a surgeon for full-time pastoral ministry. The radical nature of his sacrifice was that he earned his undergraduate degree and his medical degree from Harvard, and he has no regrets in his prophetic investment by giving of himself and his resources.

The Hammonds began Bethel in their living room with their neighbors—four adults and five children. Less than three years later the church had grown to more than three hundred Spirit-filled members, most of whom I had an opportunity to disciple during the five-year period that I served there. Bethel grew spiritually, numerically, and financially through the power of God's love and the spiritual nurturing that trickled down from the pulpit to the pews as emphasis was placed on having strong interpersonal relationships and creating a sense of belonging through fellowship, building character and community. All of these factors, according to Dr. Stewart, are the relational norms of black culture essential to the growth of black churches.[23] Due to the diversity of the congregation, even though it is an AME church, worship services on Sundays at Bethel were probably a preview of what heaven will look like with people of different races, religious backgrounds, ages, social classes, and economic statuses—red and yellow, black and white, all precious in God's sight.

The display of mutual caring, respect, and trust that is essential to church growth requires a love for God that is more than human affection. It is a decision of our wills that involves our thoughts, our intentions, and our actions. This love requires a deep commitment to change, to permit God to create within us "a pure heart," and renew within us "a steadfast spirit" (Psalm 51:10 NIV). The cleansing of hearts and the renewal of "a steadfast spirit" prepare pastors and laity to develop a spiritual holiness. This spiritual holiness culminates in social holiness for transformation and empowerment of God's people on personal and social levels. Holiness means having the God-given ability to add spiritual value—divine power—to people, places, and things of this world, in addition to living with love for God's people and God's church. Holiness that exudes love should compel the transformation of the injustices of society, especially on behalf of the poor and the oppressed.[24]

In a believer's spiritual relationship with God, we recognize our transformation into a new creature that transpires at salvation. The love of God is demonstrated by our trusting in God's divine power, loving what God loves, loving who God loves, hating what God hates, grieving over sin, and obeying God's law wholeheartedly and enthusiastically. If our relationship with the Lord is going to be deep and meaningful, loving the Lord and our neighbor must be more than a ritualistic expression or a ceremonial exercise on Sundays. It must emerge out of a heart filled with love that compels us to make the world a better place, according to Bishop Larry Kirkland.[25]

Observing how secular love affects people, we see how the word *love* has been sadly weakened and debased by its sentimental associations. We can comprehend the true meaning of love as a spiritual gift only when we keep our eyes fixed upon Christ, our crucified Savior. In John 14:15, Jesus tells us, "If you love me, you will obey what I command" (NIV). The phrase, "If you love me, you will," has gotten many women to "give it up and turn it loose," as young adults say. This is the most popular line used by teenage boys and men to get teenage girls and women to prove their love. Thus, far too many out-of-wedlock children have been conceived, shotgun weddings have been held, and abortions have been performed because of that simple phrase, which has nothing to do with love, but everything to do with lust and raging hormones.

The gospel affirms the worth and the dignity of every person, and *it seeks to bring each person into the orbit of God's power and God's love.*[26] When we desire to fulfill our selfish desires, or follow customs and convention, we defer our moral choices to others. Much of sin, racism, and materialism remains with us because it is rooted in culture or "following the crowd," and custom holds it in place. For example, the treatment of women in general, and specifically as inferiors in the church, is derived from long and tired customs that die hard. Faith in God's self-revelation in Jesus Christ causes moral judgments to be based on God's love of all humans equally, with no one being entitled to a privilege or subject to a limitation that all of us would not enjoy or suffer equally.[27] Christlike love that builds and grows churches through formation is comprised of righteousness and benevolence working in harmony. This love is not just sentiment but service and sacrifice. It is motivated not by our feelings but by our faith. It manifests itself not in emotions but in the energetic giving of ourselves that results in a constructive transformation of our spiritual lives, improving our integrity, our ethics, and our moral standards.

Conclusion

The reality of the gospel is that Christ's conception, crucifixion, and resurrection is a "love story" that began with God's salvation plan for humanity. Even though Jesus was betrayed by his closest friends, denied, and crucified by the very same people whom he came to save, his love never quit. He was obedient unto death on the cross. African American spirituality teaches black people to look to God's divine love as a source for our naming and defining our true identity and reality. Love is a centering power of African American life, which begins with our love of God and God's love of us that extends to love of self and others. Thus, we are enabled to lead a God- and Spirit-centered life.[28]

Notes

1. Carlyle Fielding Stewart III, *African American Church Growth: 12 Principles of Prophetic Ministry* (Nashville: Abingdon Press, 1994), 36.

2. Carlyle Fielding Stewart III, *God, Being, and Liberation: A Comparative Analysis of the Theologies and Ethics of James H. Cone and Howard Thurman* (Lanham, Md.: University Press of America, 1989), 213.

3. Stewart, *African American Church Growth*, 27.

4. Carlyle Fielding Stewart III, *Reclaiming What Was Lost: Recovering Spiritual Vitality in the Mainline Church* (Nashville: Abingdon Press, 2003), 21.

5. Stewart, *God, Being, and Liberation*, 149.

6. Tom Skinner, *How Black Is the Gospel?* (Philadelphia: J. B. Lippincott, 1970), 79.

7. Stewart, *African American Church Growth*, 27.

8. Martin Luther King, Jr., *Strength to Love* (1963; Philadelphia: Fortress Press, 1981), 6-7.

9. Max Lucado, *The Applause of Heaven* (Dallas: Word Publishing, 1990).

10. Henry Mitchell, *Celebration and Experience in Preaching* (Nashville: Abingdon Press, 2001).

11. Stewart, *African American Church Growth*, 40-41.

12. Carlyle Fielding Stewart III, *Black Spirituality and Black Consciousness: Soul Force, Culture, and Freedom in the African-American Experience* (Trenton, N.J.: African World Press, 1999), 66.

13. Carlyle Fielding Stewart III, *Soul Survivors: An African American Spirituality* (Louisville: Westminster John Knox Press, 1997), 34.

14. Ibid., 43.

15. Samuel DeWitt Proctor, *Preaching about Crises in the Community* (Philadelphia: Westminster Press, 1988), 34.

16. John Coltrane, *A Love Supreme,* original recording reissued by GRP Records, 1995.

17. Stewart, *Black Spirituality and Black Consciousness*, 16.

18. Robert J. Wicks, *Touching the Holy: Ordinariness, Self-Esteem, and Friendship* (Notre Dame, Ind.: Ave Maria Press, 1992).

19. Dietrich Bonhoeffer, *The Cost of Discipleship* (New York: Macmillan, 1975), 89.

20. *The AMEC Bicentennial Hymnal* (Nashville: The African Methodist Episcopal Church, 1984), 461.

21. Robert M. Franklin, *Liberating Visions: Human Fulfillment and Social Justice in African-American Thought* (Minneapolis: Fortress Press, 1990), 110-11.

22. Stewart, *African American Church Growth*, 22.

23. Ibid., 44-46.

24. Stewart, *Reclaiming What Was Lost*, 38-39.

25. Bishop Larry T. Kirkland, *Anvil: Living Well Everyday, Spiritual Relationship to God* (Nashville: African Methodist Episcopal Church Council of Bishops, 2005), 109-11.

26. Proctor, *Preaching about Crises in the Community*, 34.

27. Samuel DeWitt Proctor, *How Shall They Hear?* (Valley Forge, Pa.: Judson Press, 1992), 28.

28. Stewart, *African American Church Growth*, 52.

PART FIVE

Stewardship

CHAPTER TEN

THE ART OF GIVING

Walter L. Kimbrough

Giving is the medium by which the sacred worth of the individual is defined. We declare who we are by the way in which we give. Our personality is reflected through our established pattern of giving. What an individual values greatest in life is seen in the record of written checks. How we spend our money speaks volumes about what we treasure. Giving is a learned experience and, therefore, has to be taught to each of us at some juncture of our lives. I believe the sooner that teaching/learning takes place, the better off everyone will be.

During my seminary days, we students had to deliver a senior sermon. It was not a requirement for graduation, but it was an expectation on the part of other seminarians. This chapter takes its title from the subject of my senior sermon, which I preached nearly forty years ago. The text was taken from Mark 12:41-44 (HCSB):

> Sitting across from the temple treasury, [Jesus] watched how the crowd dropped money into the treasury. Many rich people were putting in large sums. And a poor widow came and dropped in two tiny coins worth very little. Summoning His disciples, He said to them, "I assure you: This poor widow has put in more than all

those giving to the temple treasury. For they all gave out of their surplus, but she out of her poverty has put in everything she possessed—all she had to live on."

The intent here is not to repeat the sermon but to emphasize the continuing need for people to be taught the art of giving through the preached word as well as through the traditional classroom setting. Journey with me now as we explore together the art of giving and seek to discover how our lives can be made richer and full of meaning.

We Must Be Taught to Give Early in Life

In the history of Israel, the people were directed to do an outstanding job of teaching in order to diminish the possibility of forgetting. Moses spoke with clarity to the Israelites in declaring the will of God for their lives:

> Listen, Israel: The LORD our God, the LORD is One. Love the LORD your God with all your heart, with all your soul, and with all your strength. These words that I am giving you today are to be in your heart. Repeat them to your children. Talk about them when you sit in your house and when you walk along the road, when you lie down and when you get up. Bind them as a sign on your hand and let them be a symbol on your forehead. Write them on the doorposts of your house and on your gates. (Deuteronomy 6:4-9 HCSB)

The education of our children starts in the home and cannot be wholly turned over to anyone else. Parents are to be the very first teachers of children. The Bible, then, becomes an excellent textbook. Here we find the guiding principles that will give direction, meaning, and purpose to our lives. Teach the children to give of what has been entrusted to them.

Recently, a nine-year-old boy joined our congregation along with his mother. He was and is being mentored by another member of the church who had been teaching him to be faithful in tithing. This young lad's ambition is to be on stage in the theater. As an introduction to his life's dream, he has been selected to appear in commercials for which he receives a salary. He has started out early as a tither, and as his income has increased, he has remained faithful. I believe that this boy will become a seven-digit wage earner and will continually tithe because he was taught early in life to do so. Proverbs 22:6 tells us, "Teach a youth about the way he should go; even when he is old he will not depart from it" (HCSB). The art of giving does start early in each of our lives as we have been taught by our elders. Are you the teacher, or are you the learner? One never becomes the teacher until the learning has taken place. Then, we must be faithful in not only being examples but also instructing others in the way they should go.

The story is told of another little boy who had been given two dimes before leaving the house for Sunday school. His instruction was to put one dime in the offering, and the other dime could be spent as he so desired. Instead of placing the dimes in his pocket as he walked to the church, he was throwing them up in the air and catching them as they fell down. Finally, one dime missed his hand, fell on the ground, and rolled into the sewer. He then held on tightly to the remaining dime and reverently looked upward and declared, "God, I am sorry that I lost your dime." The failure to teach the art of giving means that too many of us will become like the little boy in declaring that God's dime was lost.

Teaching our children the art of giving early in life means that we can eliminate fund-raising in the life of our congregations and major in our mandate to go and make disciples of all nations. Many years ago, the congregation I was appointed to serve as pastor agreed to a "No Fund-raising Policy." We believed that if God had blessed us with life, health, sound minds, jobs, and income, then we should give sufficiently to support the work and ministry of the Lord's church. Further, we could have in place a mechanism of supporting our colleges and universities as well as other charitable organizations. The church of Jesus Christ will then be assured of long life and vitality.

We Must Be Obedient and Faithful to the Word of God in Our Giving

The Bible is our book. It is not designed to become a collector's item. Rather, it is a book to be used as our road map to spiritual maturity. It will help us refrain from being immature, especially when we are older in years. There was a woman in the life of a congregation who gave considerably large amounts to the church without any fanfare. When asked the source of her motivation for such generous giving, she offered a simple response. She said that everywhere she read in the Bible to give, the message was clear in the same passage that she would also receive. It is true that we can never outgive God. The more we give, the more God gives to us. Jesus said, "Give, and it will be given to you; a good measure—pressed down, shaken together, and running over—will be poured into your lap. For with the measure you use, it will be measured back to you" (Luke 6:38 HCSB). We will grow in the art of giving as we develop a systematic commitment to Bible study. It is necessary to move beyond just reading the Bible to intentionally studying the Bible. The growth is intensified as one becomes involved with a serious study group. Through study, we discover that God is the principal example of excellent stewardship—the generous sharing with others of what one has without any expectation of receiving repayment from the receiver. Listen to these classic words of scripture, "For God loved the world in this way: He gave His One and Only Son, so that everyone who believes in Him will not perish, but have eternal life" (John 3:16 HCSB).

Make God Your Number One Priority in Giving

The very first commandment of God given by Moses, the great lawgiver, is, "Do not have other gods besides Me" (Deuteronomy 5:7 HCSB). The directive is plain and simple: God wants to be first in your life in everything. We must make God first and never second or even near the top in all that we do. This includes our commitment to giving. I suppose that it becomes easy to care for self first inasmuch as we have been taught that self-preservation is the first law of nature. Yet God supersedes every natural law, for there was no law prior to God. Do an inventory. Find the place of God in your living and giving.

Years ago, on a Saturday afternoon, I was visiting in the home of a parishioner. The member proudly pointed out an envelope on his nightstand that was ready to be placed in the offering plate the next morning. He indicated that if he should die during the night, God would still receive his money on time. His wife had been instructed to make sure the check was turned in to the church. When do you write your check for the offering? Is it on Saturday, or is it in haste just as the offering is being received during the worship service? I have observed some people who are consistently late in getting the offering ready. When we make God our number one priority, we always prepare in advance. We received the breath of life as a gift from God up front—in advance. God treated us not as afterthoughts but as significant parts of a divine plan; therefore, we ought to respond to him in the same way.

Give Consistently

A song that is often sung just before the offering is received during the worship service declares,

> You can't beat God giving no matter how hard you
> try.
> The more you give, the more He gives to you.

There is definitely a consistency in the giving pattern of God. Just think: the air we breathe is not a utility. It is a gift from God. Day by day there is always the presence of air in ample supply to meet our needs. God does not disappoint us, but so often we disappoint God in our failure to be faithful and consistent in giving as an act of worship.

In seeking to master the art of giving, start giving to God through the life of your local congregation on a weekly basis even if you are paid biweekly or on a monthly pension. The regularity of frequency will stimulate the habit of giving. We need to become addicted to giving. It should be as if the desire becomes an urge that is only satisfied in our active participation in the time of offering. I am always moved when worshiping in a congregation where the people get excited about the offering time. They rejoice when the offering is announced. It must be like the feeling of David as described in Psalm 122:1: "I was glad when they said unto me, let us go into the house of the LORD" (KJV). May we emulate David through giving with glad hearts and with consistency to the end that we will grow in the art of giving.

Give Generously

We serve a God of generosity. So much has been given to each one of us even when we have been unworthy to be recipients. Likewise, we have received blessings from the hands of God that we did not request. The people of old would say, "He looked beyond my faults and saw my needs." Paul tells us in 1 Corinthians 12:4-7, "Now there are different gifts, but the same Spirit. There are different ministries, but the same Lord. And there are different activities, but the same God is active in everyone and everything. A manifestation of the Spirit is given to each person to produce what is beneficial" (HCSB). Although we receive generously, we must understand that our commitment and challenge are to be productive. The issue is beyond our being faithful, for productivity must lead the way. Too many of us have taken the liberty of insisting that we have been faithful even in the midst of our nonproductivity. It is as if we have a built-in justification for failure. God desires for us to take the gifts we have received and use them for the building up of the body of Christ. Our Lord speaks with great authority in John 15:1-2, "I am the true vine, and My Father is the vineyard keeper. Every branch in Me that does not produce fruit He removes, and He prunes every branch that produces fruit so that it will produce more fruit" (HCSB). The idea of more fruit indicates that God not only expects our very best but also wants us to produce "more" fruit. A tree is known by its fruit.

Give Cheerfully

I am a firm believer that any person who is unable to give cheerfully to the Lord through the life of the church should refrain from giving. God does not need what we have in our possession. The psalmist has informed us: "The earth and everything in it, the world and its inhabitants, belong to the LORD" (Psalm 24:1 HCSB). We own nothing even though we tend to claim ownership of houses and land. Death will ultimately creep up on us, and we will leave everything for others to do as they please. A friend of mine has often declared that he has never seen an armored truck following a hearse to the cemetery. If you can't get excited about giving, just keep it.

Every person who claims to be a believer in Jesus Christ and who is active in the life of the church should intentionally study 2 Corinthians 8 and 9. Some of the most profound teaching on giving can be found in these two chapters. Every pastor should preach and teach the people from this great manuscript. Anyone selected for a position of leadership within the life of the church should seriously study this text. Therefore, I encourage you to read and then reread these chapters in order to deepen your understanding of what the art of giving is all about.

Listen to the Apostle Paul speak to our hearts in a fresh way:

> Remember this: the person who sows sparingly will also reap sparingly, and the person who sows generously will also reap generously. Each person should do as he has decided in his heart—not out of regret or out of necessity, for God loves a cheerful giver. And God is able to make every grace overflow to you, so that in every way, always having everything you need, you may excel in every good work. (2 Corinthians 9:6-8 HCSB)

Much can be derived from these words; however, they will be beneficial only when they are studied carefully, are taken to heart, and become part of your being.

Commit to Tithing as the Minimum Standard of Giving

Many pastors have taught to begin giving at a comfortable level and increase giving by 1 percent each year until the tithe level has been reached. This gives the impression that we have arrived at the height of where we ought to be in our faithfulness to the biblical mandate often quoted from the prophet Malachi: " 'Bring the full 10 percent into the storehouse so that there may be food in My house. Test Me in this way,' says the LORD of Hosts. 'See if I will not open the floodgates of heaven and pour out a blessing for you without measure' " (3:10 HCSB). God challenges us to be faithful in giving with the promise of great prosperity. It is important to give because we love God and not just because we expect to receive. The tithe should not be looked upon as the level representing completion or perfection; rather, we should consider it a beginning point. Jesus helps to clarify this in Matthew 23:23, "Woe to you, scribes and Pharisees, hypocrites! You pay a tenth of mint, dill, and cumin, yet you have neglected the more important matters of the law—justice, mercy, and faith. These things should have been done without neglecting the others" (HCSB). An understanding of the gospel lesson will move us beyond the declaration, "When praises go up, blessings come down." We cannot bribe God to bless us through our praise. He is worthy of praise on his own merit. We are blessed as a result of the favor of God and not by our acts or deeds.

Giving the Gift

I conclude this chapter on the note that the gift without the giver is bare. Let me say that another way: the greatest gift that anyone can give is the self—not money, goods, or land. I choose to give my whole being. Paul says, "Thanks be to God for His indescribable gift" (2 Corinthians 9:15).

When we give ourselves, the gift is not only indescribable; it is also priceless. Give your best with the understanding that the church and the world need you.

There are no substitutes. Jesus Christ did not have a substitute at Calvary. He had to go for himself and for our sake. He died so that we might have a right to eternal life. Perhaps the most quoted verse of scripture is John 3:16, "For God loved the world in this way: He gave His One and Only Son, so that everyone who believes in Him will not perish but have eternal life" (HCSB). I pray that you will join with me in resolving to master the art of giving the best that we have and are so that the world will be a better place in which to live and a place where Jesus Christ will be declared Lord.

Cascade: Giving and Growing

Cascade United Methodist Church was organized in 1926 as an all-white congregation. The church grew to a membership of one thousand. The Cascade community began to undergo racial transition during the decade of the 1960s and the membership began to decline. In 1974, I was the first African American pastor appointed to serve the church. At that time, the membership was less than one hundred, and the annual budget was $25,000. We used the principles of stewardship to help transform the membership and the giving to a current annual budget of $4 million.

The art of giving has been manifested as an instrument of growth in the life of Cascade through our ministry to children. We organized a children's church under the leadership of the children's pastor, who guides the worship experience. Children share in the total experience of worship geared to their level of comprehension. They are taught the meaning and significance of giving to support the work and ministries of the church. We believe that teaching strong giving principles at an early age has produced strong, caring young adults who support the life and work of Cascade. We have seen the evidence of this in the confirmation class where I am now teaching the children of my former students. Further, we teach our children the significance of saving through our youth banking center called Good Choices. This is an official Bank of America branch designed just for our children and youth, and at this time, they have in excess of $500,000 on deposit. Now, knowing how to save and to give will maintain a strong and viable Cascade.

Some years ago I discovered that persons who are students of the word of God are basically better givers. I sought to be intentional in increasing the number of Bible study classes and to offer them on a daily basis so that our people would not have an excuse for noninvolvement. This effort resulted in a hoped for increase in both giving and participation.

We were blessed in having the Reverend Wyatt T. Walker inform us about his congregation in New York—a group that majors in tithing on the part of the staff and officers. The church has truly been blessed through the emphasis on tithing. Naturally, we concluded that if God would bless these people in significant ways, then God would certainly do the same for us at Cascade. We immediately put this teaching to work, and instantly, our giving increased.

Thankfully, the art of giving at Cascade has been persistently strong. Our members are invited and encouraged to bring the tithe to the altar and leave it. This is in response to our understanding of the prophet Malachi who declared, "Bring the tithe." Some members have not been obedient to this directive; yet they tithe. They send the tithe through mail or their banks, or they bring it by the office before Sunday service. We learned from the best practices of others and made the lessons come alive for us.

Cascade is a congregation that seeks to involve every member in the life of the church. We are more prone to give when we are actively involved. Inactive people have little commitment to the well-being of the congregation. Every new members class is organized with the instruction to nurture each other and adopt a mission project as well as become involved in a ministry area of the church. Our officers are elected to serve for up to three years, and then they relinquish the position so that someone else might have an opportunity to serve.

We have not arrived at the place where we ought to be in the service of our Lord, but we are listening and learning and growing as we move forward to create a church of excellence. *To God be the glory!*

CONTRIBUTORS

Dr. Eugene A. Blair is the Director of African American Spiritual Formation and Congregational Development for the Detroit Conference of The United Methodist Church. He has served pastorates in Ohio and Illinois. He served as a missionary with the Methodist Church of Kenya, East Africa, where he taught preaching and spiritual formation at what is now known as Kenya Methodist University.

Pastor Tyrone D. Gordon is the Senior Pastor of the 5,700 member St. Luke "Community" United Methodist Church in Dallas, Texas. Pastor Gordon has written numerous articles and serves on many boards and committees in The United Methodist Church. He has served pastorates in Little Rock, Arkansas, and Wichita, Kansas, and is recognized for his emphasis on evangelism, church growth, and worship. He serves on the Board of Trustees for Philander Smith College (Little Rock, Arkansas) and St. Paul School of Theology (Kansas City, Missouri) and on the Executive Board for Perkins School of Theology at Southern Methodist University (Dallas, Texas). He is married to Marsha Douglas Gordon, and they have two beautiful daughters, Lauren and Allyson.

Rev. Walter L. Kimbrough is Senior Pastor at Cascade United Methodist Church. For more than thirty-five years, evangelism, pastoral care, teaching, preaching, and community service have characterized his ministry. He has provided leadership at all levels of The United Methodist Church in both northern Illinois and northern Georgia. After successfully leading Chicago congregations through racial transition, he was appointed in 1974 to the Cascade Church in Atlanta, Georgia. He shepherded Cascade from a dying congregation of less than 100 members to a vibrant one of more than 7,000 members. Under his leadership in 1994, the church relocated its edifice and is now preparing to relocate again to accommodate a continually growing congregation.

Dr. Les Mangum was born and raised in New York City. He was ordained elder in the Detroit Annual Conference of The United Methodist Church in 1986. He has served congregations in New York and Michigan for the last nineteen years. He is currently the Senior Pastor of St. Timothy United Methodist Church in Detroit, Michigan.

Dr. Sheron C. Patterson is the Senior Pastor of the Highland Hills United Methodist Church in Dallas, Texas, and the author of numerous books and articles. She also hosts a syndicated *Love Clinic* radio broadcast heard in fifty cities.

Dr. James C. Perkins has served as Senior Pastor of the Greater Christ Baptist Church, Detroit, Michigan, for twenty-four years. He is founder of the Benjamin E. Mays

Male Academy and Fellowship Non-Profit Housing Corporation, the community development arm of the church. Dr. Perkins is author of *Building Up Zion's Walls: Ministry for Empowering the African American Family* (Judson Press) and numerous sermons and articles in other published works. He is married and the father of two daughters.

Dr. Elston Ricky Perry has pastored five churches and served as an associate in two. These United Methodist and Baptist churches exhibited significant growth in the participation and spiritual development of African American youth and men. At present Dr. Perry is the founder of Phoenix Rising Enterprises, which emphasizes the positive development of at-risk youth and men in the San Francisco–Oakland–Bay Area. He is also a noted evangelist and workshop leader.

Dr. Vance P. Ross is Associate General Secretary of the General Board of Discipleship of The United Methodist Church.

The Rev. Dr. D. Lovett Sconiers is an ordained Elder in the African Methodist Episcopal Church (AME). She has been serving as the Chaplain, Director of Campus Ministry/Religious Life, and a Religion Professor at Edward Waters College for more than five years. She also serves as the pastor at New Bethel AME Church in White Springs, Florida, which is her fourth pastoral appointment.

Dr. J. Alfred Smith Sr. is the Senior Pastor of the Allen Temple Baptist Church in Oakland, California. He also serves as Professor of Christian Ministry and Preaching at the American Baptist Seminary of the West in Berkeley, California. For two years, he was one of *Ebony's* "100 Most Influential Black Americans," and was among *Ebony's* "Top 15 Greatest Black Preachers of 1993." In 2001, Dr. Smith was awarded the Lifetime Achievement Award by the Greenlining Institute and the Humanitarian of the Year Award by East Bay Agency for Children; and in 2002, the Agape Award from the Women's Ministry of Shiloh Baptist Church, Washington, D.C., and the Gandhi Ikeda Award from Morehouse College. He is the author of sixteen books; his most recent book, *On the Jericho Road* (2004), is the story of his life in ministry. Dr. Smith is a past president of the Progressive National Baptist Convention (PNBC) and the American Baptist Churches of the West (ABCW). He is married to JoAnna Goodwin Smith, is the father of three sons and two daughters, and has fourteen grandchildren and five great-grandchildren.

The Reverend Dr. Jeremiah A. Wright Jr. became Pastor of Trinity United Church of Christ (TUCC) on March 1, 1972, and has been Senior Pastor for more than thirty-three years. He holds a Doctor of Ministry degree from United Theological Seminary, a master's degree from Howard University, an additional master's degree from the University of Chicago Divinity School, and seven honorary doctorate degrees. He has lectured at many seminaries and universities in the nation, and has represented Trinity and the United Church of Christ around the world. Under Dr. Wright's leadership, Trinity Church has grown from 200 to more than 8,500 active members and has been supporting missions in Ghana, West Africa, and in Durban, South Africa, for more than a decade. The Ga Dangme people of Ghana honored Pastor Wright with the name Chief Afotey Oblum II. He is recognized as a leading theologian and pastor and has published four books and numerous articles. He shares his life with his wife, Ramah Reed Wright, and he is the father of four daughters: Janet Marie Moore, Jeri Wright-Harris, Nikol D. Reed, and Jamila Nandi Wright; and one son, Nathan D. Reed. He is also the grandfather of three grandchildren: Jeremiah Antonio Haynes, Jazmin Lynne Hall, and Steven L. Moore Jr.